The radical imagination

About the authors

MAX HAIVEN is an assistant professor in the Division of Art History and Critical Studies at the Nova Scotia College of Art and Design and co-director of the Radical Imagination Project (radicalimagination.org). He is author of *Crises of Imagination, Crises of Power: Capitalism, Creativity and the Commons* (Zed Books, 2014) and *Cultures of Financialization: Fictitious Capital in Popular Culture and Everyday Life*. More information can be found at maxhaiven.com.

ALEX KHASNABISH is an associate professor in the Department of Sociology/Anthropology at Mount Saint Vincent University and co-director of the Radical Imagination Project (radicalimagination.org). He is the author of *Zapatistas: Rebellion from the Grassroots to the Global* (Zed Books, 2010) and *Zapatismo beyond Borders*, and co-editor (with Jeffrey Juris) of *Insurgent Encounters: Transnational Activism, Ethnography, and the Political*. More information can be found at alexkhasnabish.com.

The radical imagination

Social movement research in the age of austerity

MAX HAIVEN AND ALEX KHASNABISH

Fernwood Publishing | HALIFAX & WINNIPEG

Zed Books | LONDON

The Radical Imagination: Social Movement Research in the Age of Austerity
was first published in 2014

Published in Canada by Fernwood Publishing,
32 Oceanvista Lane, Black Point, Nova Scotia, B 0J 1B0 and
748 Broadway Avenue, Winnipeg, Manitoba, R3G 0X3

www.fernwoodpublishing.ca

Published in the rest of the world by Zed Books Ltd,
7 Cynthia Street, London N1 9JF, UK

www.zedbooks.co.uk

Typeset in Monotype Bembo by illuminati, Grosmont
Index by John Barker
Cover designed by www.stevenmarsden.com

Fernwood Publishing Company Limited gratefully acknowledges the
financial support of the Government of Canada through the Canada
Book Fund and the Canada Council for the Arts, the Nova Scotia
Department of Communities, Culture and Heritage, the Manitoba
Department of Culture, Heritage and Tourism under the Manitoba Book
Publishers Marketing Assistance Program and the Province of Manitoba,
through the Book Publishing Tax Credit, for our publishing program.

A catalogue record for this book is available from the British Library
Library of Congress Cataloging in Publication Data available
Library and Archives Canada Cataloguing in Publication data available

ISBN 978-1-78032-902-4 hb (Zed Books)
ISBN 978-1-78032-901-7 pb (Zed Books)
ISBN 978-1-55266-693-7 pb (Fernwood Publishing)

Contents

Acknowledgements

Our greatest thanks go to all those who collaborated on this research in Halifax, Nova Scotia. While they are too numerous to name, we are extremely grateful to all the activists and organizers who gave of their time and energies to make this project a success. Special thanks also go to our research assistants James Babbitt and River Smith, as well as Chris Dixon, Richard Day, Pierre Loiselle, Gary Kinsman, Jamie Yard and Sandra Jeppesen. Thanks also to Ken Barlow, Kika Sroka-Miller, our anonymous reviewers, and everyone at Zed Books, who supported this project and helped bring it to fruition. And, of course, a very special thanks to our families without whom none of this would be possible. We also acknowledge the vital financial support for this project provided by the Social Sciences and Humanities Research Council of Canada and Mount Saint Vincent University.

The importance of the radical imagination in dark times

This is a book about the radical imagination as it plays out in radical social movements today. Part history, part ethnography, part social theory, and part insurgent knowledge production, these pages seek to tease out what makes resistance tick in a world of crisis. The neocolonial 'War on Terror' and the financial meltdown have served as pretext for ushering in a ruthless global austerity agenda backed by increased military presence and police force. In this moment, the need for the radical imagination and for robust and militant social movements is more pressing than ever. It is no exaggeration to say that the situation is dire. We are amidst what Patrick Reinsborough (2010) has called a 'slow motion apocalypse' where global capitalism has unleashed a gradually unfolding collection of cascading crises: ecological collapse; energy, food and water shortages; humanitarian nightmares in war zones, neocolonial exploitation zones and disaster capitalist 'sacrifice zones'; and the less tangible but no less terrifying growth of massive social alienation and dislocation, along with its cruel medicines – militarism, addictions, fundamentalisms, racism, xenophobia and social violence. If ever there was a need for the radical imagination and social movements to materialize it, it is now.

In these times, no research is neutral. We join many others in insisting that social movement research is not merely the work of distanced data collection and interpretation, but an intimate and vital part of social transformation. But, unlike many, we take seriously the question of the researcher's responsibility not merely to 'observe' and report on the radical imagination but to awaken, enliven and 'convoke' it. This book, then, sees research not as a foreign presence within social movements, but as an important part of the way social movements reproduce themselves. We argue that the processes of 'research' are already under way in social movements, and that researchers can arrive not simply as outside observers, but as critical, reflexive agents who work in solidarity with movements to build their capacity for resilient and transformative struggle.

In this sense, this is a book for those involved in social movements, a book for those who admire social movements, a book for those who seek to understand social movements, and a book for all those fascinated by the radical imagination. Our aim is to show that the radical imagination remains a driving force in the dynamics of our political moment, that it is not an individual possession but a collective process, and that social movements depend on it to navigate our rapidly changing times.

What is the radical imagination?

The radical imagination is a term employed by many and explored by few. It evokes in us the notion of the capacity to think critically, reflexively and innovatively about the social world, and yet it eludes definition. It is, ultimately, an aspirational term, largely hollow of any concrete content or meaning. But for all that, it is vital in an age when the world has been commandeered by the grim, merciless and zombie-like ideology of austerity (Blythe 2013; Haiven 2011a; Leger 2013). In spite of the fact that practically no one still believes in the emancipatory and uplifting power of free markets, the neoliberal paradigm has been given a hideous afterlife in the wake of the 2007/8 financial collapse and today preoccupies what we imagine is and is not possible (Fisher 2009; McNally 2012). While all too often the idea of the radical imagination is scoffed at as an ephemeral, intangible and woolly feel-good slogan that distracts us from the 'real' work of social justice, we argue here that it is real and important and that we ignore and belittle it at our peril.

On the surface level, the radical imagination is the ability to imagine the world, life and social institutions not as they are but as they might otherwise be. It is the courage and the intelligence to recognize that the world can and should be changed. But the radical imagination is not just about dreaming of different futures. It's about bringing those possible futures 'back' to *work* on the present, to inspire action and new forms of solidarity today. Likewise, the radical imagination is about drawing on the past, telling different stories about how the world came to be the way it is, and remembering the power and importance of past struggles and the way their spirits live on in the present (see Haiven 2011b). The radical imagination is also about imagining the present differently too. It represents our capacity to imagine and make common cause with the experiences of other people; it undergirds our capacity to build solidarity across boundaries and borders, real or imagined. Without the radical imagination, we are left only with the residual dreams of the powerful, and for the vast majority they are not experienced as dreams but as nightmares of insecurity, precarity, violence and hopelessness. Without the radical imagination, we are lost.

We approach the radical imagination not as a thing that individuals *possess* in greater or lesser quantities but as a collective *process*, something that groups *do* and do together (see also Haiven and Khasnabish 2010). We understand the imagination as our capacity to think about those things we do not or cannot directly experience, but it is also the filter or the frame through which we interpret our own experiences (see Haiven 2014). For this reason, the imagination is an intimate part of how we empathize with others, the way we gain some sense of the forces that impact our lives, and the way we project ourselves into the future and gain inspiration and direction from the past. Yet, contrary to many applications of the idea, we understand the imagination as not merely the 'private property' of the individual. Through shared experiences, language, stories, ideas, art and theory we share part of our imagination. We create, with those around us, multiple, overlapping, contradictory and coexistent imaginary landscapes, horizons of common possibility and shared understanding. These shared landscapes are shaped by and also shape the imaginations and the actions of their participant individuals.

We can 'conjugate' the idea of the imagination into several different overlapping 'tenses'. On the one hand, we can still talk about the imagination in the ways we are accustomed – as a conscious creative force of the individual mind – so long as we note that the borders of that imagination are never sharp, that the imaginative capacity of any individual is influenced by and influences others. We can also talk about shared 'imaginaries': broad sets or landscapes of shared understandings and narratives that make living together possible. So, for instance, we can speak about nations as imagined communities, and more broadly the way arbitrary borders between individuals are created and reinforced through common cultural referents and social institutions (see Anderson 2006; Appadurai 1996; Taylor 2004). Finally, as we shall discuss shortly, we can also speak of the imagination in a more psychoanalytic and philosophical frame, as a deep force at the very basis of the human subject, the realm of 'the imaginary' (*l'imaginaire*) where ideas, meanings, associations, fixations, drives and affects circulate beneath the threshold of conscious thought (see Urribarri 2002). These three 'tenses' of the idea of the imagination are intertwined and interreliant.

The notion of the 'radical imagination' relies on a second term. The notion of the 'radical' inherits its most powerful meaning from the Latin *radix* or 'root', in the sense that radical ideas, ideologies or perspectives are informed by the understanding that social, political, economic and cultural problems are outcomes of deeply rooted tensions, contradictions, power imbalances, and forms of oppression and exploitation. As a result, radicalism does not so much describe a certain set of tactics, strategies or beliefs but rather speaks to a general understanding that even if 'the system' as a whole can be changed through gradual institutional reforms, those reforms must be based on and aimed at a transformation of the fundamental qualities and tenets of the system itself. The idea of 'radicalism' cannot be monopolized by any point on the political spectrum: fundamentalists, far-right militias, neoconservative pundits and others also display elements of radicalism as much as (sometimes more than) the anticapitalist organizers, anti-racist activists, feminist campaigners, or independent journalists, critical academics and writers who make up the cast of characters in this book.

In this sense, we, like philosopher Cornelius Castoriadis, use the term 'radical imagination' less as a value judgement and more to refer to an analytic category or sociological process. For Castoriadis (1997), who sought to combine the insights of Freudian psychoanalysis with the lessons of Marxism, the radical imagination is that tectonic, protean substance out of which all social institutions and identities are made, and which, likewise, is constantly in motion under the surface of society, undermining and challenging all that we take to be real, hard, fast and eternal (see also Urrabarri 2002). Likening the radical imagination to magma, that volcanic substance between liquid and solid, Castoriadis suggests that seemingly permanent social forms (from the ideal of marriage to the form of the state, from the value of money to the concept of the nation) are the temporary solidifications of the (shared) radical imagination. After all, these all-too-powerful institutions are, ultimately, imaginary ideas given real power by the way they influence our social actions and relationships (see also Graber 2001). But that very substance out of which they are wrought also erodes their foundations: the radical imagination is also that force within us as individuals and collectives that resists the present order, that, to paraphrase John Holloway (2002), screams 'no!' and refuses to be conscripted.

But, as Marcel Stoezler and Nira Yuval-Davis (2002) caution us, the radical imagination is no one universal thing. Rather, the imagination is shaped by our experience as embodied subjects who are intersected by race, class, gender, sexuality, nationality, ethnicity and other differences. Indeed, as Justin Paulson (2010) notes, on a phenomenological level the imagination is the product of difference: it is sparked and grows when we encounter the unexpected, the foreign, the new.

With these theoretical signposts in mind, in this book we want to move away from the idea of the radical imagination as a hollow slogan based on some essential idea. We don't seek to define what the radical imagination *is*, but to investigate the way the radical imagination *works*. In order to make such an approach to the radical imagination a practical means by which we can understand social movements (the purpose of this book), we can begin by making a few observations.

The first is that social movements are *convocations* of the radical imagination: they are convened by individuals who share some understanding of the world in a radical sense – that is, in the sense that they see the problems they confront as deeply rooted in societal institutions and, importantly, believe these institutions can and should be changed. While social movements may be many things and take many forms, we suggest that at least one aspect of all these manifestations is the (sometimes intentional, sometimes incidental) cultivation of common imaginary landscapes, but this cultivation is an active process, not a steady state.

So, second, social movements are animated by the movement of the radical imagination. This is not to say that all members inhabit identical imaginary landscapes, but rather that the driving dynamic of social movements is the tensions and conflicts and dialogues between imaginative actors. The radical imagination is no static thing to be studied under the microscope or measured through quantitative analysis. It must be observed as it 'sparks' from the friction between individuals, groups, ideas, strategies and tactics.

Finally, social movement researchers should not satisfy themselves with merely observing the radical imagination at play in social movements. Rather, as we argue, they should seek to 'convoke' it. That is, researchers must see themselves, their research and their writing as intimate parts of the way social movements *reproduce* themselves. Rather than shy away from having an impact or disturbing movement equilibriums, social movement researchers, in highly reflexive, responsive and responsible ways, should see themselves as part of the play of the radical imagination.

Social movements in the age of austerity

In Chapter 3, we characterize social movements as caught between two or more spheres of 'reproduction'. Borrowing a term from Marxist feminist analysis, reproduction here means more than the biological business of bearing children. Rather, it speaks to the way social life is 'reproduced' more broadly, and the way capitalism itself is reproduced through a pattern of endless crisis (Federici 2012; Mies 1986; Weeks 2011). We understand social movements and the radical imagination as caught in a contradiction. On the one hand, social movements inherently envision and seek to bring about a fundamental change in the way society is reproduced. In other words, whether they seek to change government policy, institutional and organizational systems, or cultural norms, movements do not want society to be reproduced in its current form. This is especially, but not exclusively, the case for radical social movements that see the problems they face as deeply rooted in the social order, and recognize that a radical change to the social order is necessary if these problems are to be solved.

On the other hand, however, whether intentionally or not, social movements also become zones or spheres of alternative social reproduction for their participants. They become spaces of identity formation, friendship, meaning, care and possibility, though, as we shall see, they are never unproblematic utopias (far from it). They often seek to create, within their organizational form or norms, a paradigmatic living alternative to the society they seek to change, a tendency that has become much more conscious and common since the rise of 'new social movements' over the last forty years, and especially so since the 'anarchist turn' in the 1990s (Day 2005) (see Chapter 5).

Focusing on this tension reveals a number of dynamics we and others have observed or experienced in social movement research. In Chapter 4, for instance, we address this tension at length, using it to unpack the question of movement 'failure' and 'success' and the way movements keep the radical imagination alive in dark times. In Chapter 6, we explore this tension as it plays out in the reproduction of oppression within radical social movements. And in Chapter 8 we explore the way researchers can reimagine themselves when working with social movements amidst crises of reproduction.

We pay attention to this tension because, to a very real extent, the crisis of social reproduction in global capitalist society at large is intensifying on at least three fronts. The ramping up of neoliberalism in the form of an unapologetic and vicious austerity regime has seen the further subjugation of governments to the will of capital and the evisceration of what remained of the welfare state (McNally 2012). As government services (health, education, transportation, regulatory bodies, corporate oversight, etc.) are slashed or privatized, society becomes increasingly individualized and financialized, with increasingly isolated individuals left to fend for themselves against the vicissitudes of the market (Giroux 2012). Second, the 'War on Terror' continues to justify the amplification of repression, surveillance, war and policing around the world, and has fortified a culture of fear backed by racist fantasies and neocolonial ambitions (Brown 2010; Mohanty 2003; Razack 2008). Third, the deepening ecological crisis – notably the increasing toxicity of the environment and climate chaos unleashed by global warming – threaten to set loose yet unimagined terrors on the world's populations, terrors that will likely be suffered and endured most intensively by the poor and marginalized as governments and communities continue to be dismantled and capitalist impunity is enshrined (Foster, Clark and York 2010). The sum of these factors is a wholesale global crisis of social reproduction, where social life itself is made to pay the cost of the reproduction of a renegade capitalist system (Federici 2012; Haiven 2014; McMurtry 2013). This crisis manifests in part as the intensification of fundamentalisms, prejudices and hatreds, as well as a retreat further into competitive individualism and consumerism (Giroux 2012).

In these times, when the majority of individuals in the anglophone North Atlantic live increasingly isolated lives, social movements are not merely important as vehicles for patently necessary social change. They become islands of refuge in a tempestuous world. In their organizational forms and group norms, they often 'prefigure' the world they would like to see, one that values individuality and communality, democracy and solidarity, equality and acceptance, passion and reason, hope and love. They often serve as spaces of friendship, community, romance and empowerment. This is true even of those more severe and formal organizations and groups that strictly disavow their social dimensions.

If the radical imagination is something we *do* together, then we cannot disavow the capacity of social movements to foster alternative spaces and times of social reproduction. The building of rich relationships and pluralistic organizational forms is an important part of struggling to overcome the crisis of social reproduction under which we all labour. Yet, at the same time, we and others have observed that movements and activists all too often fall prey to the crises of reproduction *within* their own organizations and movements. Sometimes this manifests as open conflicts over strategy and tactics. At other times (indeed, we'd suggest, usually) it manifests as personality conflicts or social tensions. Frequently, both of these are the result of the way the movement or group in question continues to reproduce the oppressive behaviours or patterns it has inherited from the society of which it is a part (see Chapter 6).

And so, borrowing a term from the Edu-factory Collective (2009), we want to identify contemporary social movements as the site of a 'double crisis'. On the one hand, they exist within a society in the paroxysms of a massive, universal crisis of reproduction which, while it is experienced at different levels of intensity by different people depending on race, class, gender, sexuality, citizenship, (dis)ability and other forms of oppression, is experienced by everyone. On the other hand, movements themselves contend with a crisis of reproduction within their own forms, organizations and milieus. This double crisis is the context of the radical imagination today.

Research as enclosure and as commons

The idea of the radical imagination and the concept of the double crisis of social movements in an age of austerity, we suggest, help us to reimagine social movement research. As Stefano Harney and Fred Moten (2013) explain, 'research' is a term often monopolized by the academy, which presumes to hold the exclusive rights to the process through its disciplinary architecture. But these authors rightly point out that research and rigorous inquiry are an intimate part of everyday life, and especially an important part of life as it is experienced through struggles against systemic power. Both as individuals and as collectives, we are constantly gathering information, processing it, and using the results of inquiry to form a common agenda for change. For Moten and Harney, the university is an artificial and historically particular institution that devalues certain forms of research (the everyday sort) and exalts others (the highly disciplined, academic sort). But it is also, for them, a space of possibility, animated by the activity of what they call the 'undercommons', that network of radical alliances and solidarities that undergird academe, those insiders and outsiders who, against the tide of elitism, enclosure, privatization, commercialization and disciplinary pressure, seek to mobilize the unique historical location and material power of the university to imagine and build a world beyond the present order.

In this spirit, we want to imagine a form of social movement research that is not primarily about the generation of 'academic capital': those forms of publication and information management that are valued by the powers that be and are the currency for entrance to their ranks. Such an approach is in stark contrast to the origins of social movement studies in the pathologization of popular resistance and social change struggles (see Chapter 1) or even to many of the current trends in social movement research that largely seek to transform and translate social movements into unintelligible academic jargon for the purposes of publication, with the ultimate material benefit (jobs, tenure, promotions, etc.) accruing to the researcher. At its worst, this sort of research represents an 'enclosure' of common social movement research: the movement in question does the hard work of reproducing itself based on its own internal processes of imagining and reflecting; the researcher swoops in, applies a disciplinary lens, collects 'data', takes what he or she needs to generate new grist for the academic mill, and leaves.

We liken this process to 'enclosure' to draw a parallel between the animus of academe and the modus operandi of capital. The idea of the enclosure draws on the history of what Marx called 'primitive accumulation', the initial stage of capitalist exploitation which, between the 1500s and the 1800s, saw the Western European ruling class systematically strip the peasantry of their common lands and property through a combination of legal, economic and military manoeuvres (Perelman 2000; Thompson 1968). This process was known, in general, as 'enclosure' because it saw common lands and resources literally 'enclosed' by fences and ditches to demarcate it as private property. These now-dispossessed people became the working class who, denied their means of reproducing themselves autonomously, were forced to sell their labour power for a wage, or were the cannon-fodder of European colonial expansion. For authors including Silvia Federici (2003), Massimo De Angelis (2007), Peter Linebaugh (2009) and George Caffentzis (2013), as well as the Midnight Notes Collective (1992), this process of the enclosure of the commons is also a potent metaphor and model for the central motive force behind capitalism even today. They understand capitalism as a struggle not only over wages and working conditions but also over the possibility of creating new commons, and the enclosure of those commons by capital. The privatization of the welfare state, for instance, or the transformation of reproductive labour into the 'service sector' are both examples of the way capitalism expands and restructures itself through new enclosures. But so, too, is the privatization of water, the toxification of the environment, the increasing surveillance and securitization of the Internet and the processes variously called 'accumulation by dispossession' (Harvey 2003) and 'disaster capitalism' (Klein 2008) where corporations and governments exploit disasters to privatize social wealth and infrastructure. As autonomist Marxists (Dyer-Witheford 1999; Hardt and Negri 2000, 2004, 2011; Holloway 2002; Virno 2003) have done well to point out, capital is a parasite living off 'living labour' that is always, ultimately, done in common.

From this perspective, we can understand the disciplinary capture of social movement knowledges through certain forms of academic research as a form of enclosure. Linda Tuhiwai Smith (2012), among others, has written about the way colonialism is enacted in part through the reduction of Indigenous people and their cultures and practices to objects of study, a process wherein Indigenous knowledge and intellectual work are seized and incorporated by colonial knowledge systems in order to better police and subjugate their progenitors. Likewise, the recent tide of 'biopiracy' – where Indigenous medicines or seeds, developed sometimes over aeons of Indigenous research, are patented and commodified by transnational corporations – is an example of the enclosure of common research (Shiva 1997). As Shawn Wilson (2009) illustrates, Indigenous research is often misrecognized as ceremony, story and discussion because it is deeply folded into the practices of everyday life and the reproduction of community. This misrecognition allows colonial researchers to 'enclose' this common research with impunity and is based on (and reinforces) the Eurocentric belief that only modern Western culture possesses the reflexivity, rigour and discipline to generate reliable or valuable knowledge.

We can understand the practice of conventional social movement research as part of this trajectory of enclosure. While researchers may believe they are simply observing and recording the facts about a given social movement, they are, in our opinion, often gaining the benefit of the 'research' process that movements are always-already conducting. This everyday 'research' takes the form of a constant experimentation and reflexive refinement of political ambitions, organizational norms, forms of democracy, institutional structures and social reproduction. While movements don't typically call this common work 'research', we hold that thinking about it as such is crucial if we are to better understand and reimagine the radical imagination and social movement research strategies.

Of course, many researchers are drawn to social movements because they sympathize with them and seek to work 'with' (rather than 'on') activists and activism. We characterize most of these efforts at solidarity-based research as falling into two camps, or being animated by two strategies (see Chapter 1). The strategy of 'invocation' tends to mobilize traditional disciplinary techniques (ethnography, statistical analysis, sociological methods, etc.) in order to gain information on and insight into movements in order to publish materials that are imagined either to be useful to movements (such as a survey of similar movements across jurisdictions, or an explanation of the legal and governmental structures movements face, or a historicization and contextualization of the movement) or that will valorize and legitimate the movement in the eyes of outsiders. We call this a strategy of 'invocation' because the researcher here invokes the presence of the movement in their work, mobilizing the (limited, but significant) privilege and power of the academic researcher to bring positive attention and recognition to the importance of the struggle in question.

Alternately, many researchers have pursued a strategy of 'avocation' or calling-away-from. Here the researcher seeks to put their privilege and power directly in the hands of the movement in question, seeking direction from and sometimes disappearing into the movement. This might take the form, for instance, of putting one's methodological discipline at the disposal of the movement, doing research on corporations under scrutiny, environmental impacts of development, or the historical precedents of a given struggle. We call this strategy 'avocation' because it might be seen as a retreat from or a rejection of the unjust privilege and power of the academic researcher.

Both of these strategies are crucial, and we, in the course of this project and others, have mobilized both. Yet in an attempt to think through the implications of the radical imagination and the double crisis of movement reproduction, we wanted to experiment with a third strategy, one we call 'convocation'. To convoke is to call together, and with this idea in mind we wanted to imagine a form of research that would seek to awaken, sharpen and enliven movements' inherent capacities for 'research' in the broader sense that Harney and Moten (2013) articulate: a process of critical self-reflection, of locating oneself and one's struggles within the multiple intersections of power, and of change and transformation. A strategy of convocation neither makes an academic fetish of social movements, nor throws away the strange, unjust and problematic privilege of the academic researcher. Rather, it seeks to mobilize our historic circumstances and privileges to provide for movements something that they, all too often, tend to bypass or take for granted. We wanted to use our power as researchers to create new spaces of dialogue, debate, reflection, questioning and empowerment. In other words, and as we discuss more fully in Chapter 8, we wanted to imagine and experiment with what 'prefigurative' research might look like, a form of research borrowed from a post-revolutionary future. We wanted to imagine a form of 'common' research, beyond enclosure.

Learning from failure

A few years ago, we sought to invent this new strategy as a response to the context in which our research took place, as all solidarity researchers must. Halifax is a small city (with a metropolitan population of roughly 400,000, with around 70,000 living in the heart of the city) on Canada's East Coast, an area of the country with a long history of workers' struggles but also one that has fallen on hard times since the decline of shipping (in the nineteenth century) and fishery (in the late twentieth century), and certainly since the deindustrialization germane to post-Cold War globalization. Halifax is the largest city in the Atlantic provinces and a regional government, military, health-care and academic hub (with more universities per capita than any city in Canada) and is, as a result and in spite of its relative poverty compared to other Canadian cities, an island of prosperity in a province and region that boasts some of the worst poverty in the country. For all that, Halifax remains a city blighted by poverty, debt and racialized injustice.

Here was a site where social movements and the radical imagination were, by all accounts, in remission. In 2010, when we commenced the research project, the activist community had recently suffered a major fissure in the wake of protests against a summit of Canadian and American political and business elites seeking to extend the neoliberal agenda through a regional trade agreement. The protest mobilization had become split along lines that are predictable to many seasoned activists and social movement scholars: tensions between those who wished to stage vociferous but 'peaceful' opposition and those who advocated various forms of 'direct action', largely confined to altercations with police and limited corporate property damage. The latter resulted in multiple arrests and a great deal of public outrage towards protesters, and subsequently huge rifts in the city's activist milieu. These rifts were to deepen after the mainstream political party furthest to the left (the

New Democratic Party) swept to victory in the 2010 provincial election, thanks in part to decades of selfless volunteer labour by activists and organizers. Once elected, they (predictably) proceeded to freeze radical voices out of the party and govern with a shamefaced neoliberal orientation. Meanwhile, several established groups in the Halifax radical milieu had recently collapsed or been eclipsed, and several prominent organizers had moved away, something quite common in the transient port city. By the time we began our research, there was a palpable tone of pessimism and fatalism in local movements.

We discuss the Halifax situation in more detail in Chapter 2, as well as our research methodologies. For now we want to point out that our ambition to develop a strategy of 'convocation' responded to several factors in our research community. First, it was a response to the fact that the Halifax social movement milieu was highly fragmented, with many activists coming and going, and many belonging to multiple overlapping (sometimes contradictory) organizations at once. Second, it was a response to the realization that movements in the city were at a nadir in terms of energy, optimism and organizational fortitude. While some robust, cohesive movements often do create spaces of reflection, research and reproduction, Halifax movements typically (though with some exceptions) lacked this capacity when we began. Third, we wanted to work in a community that, in terms of its role in global and even national affairs, was relatively marginal and marginalized.

All too often researchers seek out the most robust, successful, inspiring and exceptional movements for study. This, we argue in Chapter 4, is the result of a certain addiction to a romantic narrative of social movement and research 'success'. Instead, we wanted to dwell within and learn from what might appear at first as failure, stagnation and disorganization.

The true life of the radical imagination, like the life of each of us, is not made up of the moments of success and triumph. It is made up of the everyday work of reproducing life, of dwelling at what might at first appear to be the cusp of failure. The production of what Yves Femion (2002) calls 'orgasms of history', moments when social movements actually succeed and rupture or transform the flows of social reproduction, are no doubt important. But equally important is the routine, banal and often heart-wearying labour of reproducing the radical imagination in what we call (in Chapter 3) the 'hiatus': the long winter of dwelling between success and failure. And for us, the role of the social movement researcher should be reconceived to reflect this importance, not only in terms of how we explain and understand movements, but how we seek to work in solidarity with them.

Outline and preliminaries

The book is divided into four sections and eight chapters.

Chapter 1 parses the history of social movements studies and the politics of the university and of knowledge production. We argue that, in contrast to conventional approaches to 'social movements studies' which seek to isolate and analyse radical actors as if they were objective social phenomena to be quantified or explained, we must take up the lessons of militant ethnography, which centres movement knowledge production and a close relationship between researchers and movements, as a means to gain a deeper understanding of the radical imagination. We locate the controversies and debates about social movement research amidst a university in the grips of a massive neoliberal crisis, one which leaves little room for the myths of scholarly neutrality.

We conclude Chapter 1 by suggesting that attempts at 'solidarity research' generally fit into two camps: those of 'invocation' (attempts to use scholarly privilege to valorize movements) and those of 'avocation' (attempts to put scholarly privilege in the service of social movements directly). In contrast, in Chapter 2 we outline our research strategy of 'convocation', an attempt to bring social movement actors together in new forms of dialogue and debate. We explain why we imagined such a strategy to be necessary for working with social movements in Halifax and delve in more detail into the question and potential of the radical imagination and the ways we might both study it and mobilize it as a militant and radical concept.

Chapters 3 and 4 ask us to rethink the categories of success and failure as they relate to social movements and to social movement research. In Chapter 3 we suggest that, in the shadow of the double crisis of social reproduction, we need to understand social movements as dwelling in the 'hiatus' between success and failure. This means that the criteria for 'successful' research need to be re-examined and reimagined. Drawing on critical and queer theory, in Chapter 4 we suggest that the ideal of 'success' may do more harm than good, and may contribute to the high incidence of activist burnout that diminishes movements' ability to transform the world.

In Chapter 5 we continue to explore the double crisis of social reproduction by looking at the lives of the radical left in the anglophone North Atlantic and the reproduction of oppression within social movements. In Chapter 6, parsing the literature on anti-oppression politics, we suggest that social movements need to reject a self-congratulatory liberal politics of 'making space' for diversity and embrace a more radical (but harder and possibly endless) process of 'making time' to confront and overcome oppression.

In Chapters 7 and 8 we conclude the book by further elaborating the synchronicity between academic research methods and social movement reproduction. We offer a sketch of what we imagine as 'prefigurative research', a research methodology that is borrowed from the future we wish to create. In Chapter 7 we take up the well-known research paradigm which encourages scholars to align their ontology, epistemology and methodology and map it onto social movement practice, shedding light on the relationship between the imagination, strategies and tactics. In Chapter 8 we call for a research methodology that dedicates itself to animating, enlivening and awakening the radical imagination by creating new spaces and times of dialogue and debate, spaces where movements might 'research' themselves and their historical and social locations as part of a reflexive project of transforming social reproduction, both on the level of society at large and on the level of movement organization, culture and subjectivity.

As might be evident from this overview, this book is not strictly ethnographic in nature, though the project of which it is a part has relied upon ethnographic methods. It does not provide a deep analysis of a community under study. We have sought to write a book about the radical imagination as it is being summoned into being by people struggling to change their world, not one that offers a snapshot of movements in a specific location and at a particular moment in time. Indeed, while the context of our Halifax research project is central to this book, we have chosen to write a much more general book of reflections, observations and theorizations based upon our experience as social movement participant-researchers in the hope of contributing to a wider conversation capable of continuing to convoke the radical imagination in dark times. Deeply informing this approach is our study of globalization, social power, social movement studies, critical theory, cultural studies, anthropology, and a plurality of movement literatures ranging from liberation theology to anarchism, from Marxism to feminism to queer theory. It is a book about the radical imagination, informed by, but not limited to, the context of its emergence.

The limitations of this book are many and we freely admit to them. As mentioned above, and as we shall revisit throughout this book, the imagination is not some transcendental spirit but an embodied presence. As such, our own imaginations are constrained by our circumstances and experiences. We are both read by society as white, hetero- and cis-sexual able-bodied men. We are uninvited settlers on unceded Indigenous Mi'Kmaq land. We both have Ph.D.s and (as of writing) permanent academic jobs affording us the debt-fuelled illusion of middle-class lifestyles. While we both have backgrounds in radical activism, and while neither of us was raised in a wealthy household, we have been relatively insulated from the massive personal costs of neoliberal capitalism. We are both parents, but our children do not feel material privation and we do not fear that, by virtue of their race or class, they will be targeted by police or will be unduly likely to fall prey to violence.

We account here for our privileges not out of a politics of apology but to situate ourselves and this work. In the course of our research the choices we made, the voices we heard, the participants we engaged, and the literature we consulted were unavoidably influenced by the way our situated identities and bodies were habituated and oriented towards certain imaginative patterns. The imagination is not forever and always bound by the limits of experience, but, as Stoezler and Yuval-Davis (2002) note, and as we illustrate in Part Three of this book, the labour of imagining beyond one's own situatedness is difficult and never finished. The expansion of the imagination is the work of solidarity, and solidarity is, in part, a broadening of the imagination. We have done our best here to make the persistence of oppression central to our understanding of social movements and the radical imagination, but there remains much work to do.

In writing and researching this book we were forced to draw lines around concepts like 'radicalism', 'social movements', and 'activism' that we acknowledge from the outset are blurry. As mentioned above, 'radicalism' does not only describe the forms of thought and feeling with which we sympathize – it can also characterize groups and perspectives we have little time for or loathe (such as free-market libertarianism, bellicose nationalism, religious fundamentalism or organized racism). Equally, we can find radicalism in the much more subtle and quiet modes of resistance and refusal that are usually ignored by the media, by society and by researchers. Many forms of everyday activism and resistance fly under the radar of this study and others. In our focus on social movements (even while we define 'movements' broadly, and included in our research many who worked for NGOs, taught at universities, volunteered at shelters, and otherwise engaged in less conventionally activist-esque activities), we had to exclude many of those ways that resistance to capitalism and oppression occur on the level of everyday life, on the level of individual personality, or on the level of community survival.

Yet these forms of resistance are not insignificant. If, as we claim in this book, social movements are, in part, alternative modes and spaces of social reproduction, experimental zones where the imagination of who and what is valuable might reject convention and be built from the ground up, then what we missed in this research might well have been the best examples and the most salient and powerful models of resistance and alternative-building. But an engagement with them will need to wait for a later time. And, in spite of their importance, we are still of the belief that to create meaningful and lasting social change both the conventional social movements we examined and all the spheres of everyday resistance we missed will need, somehow, to develop a degree of organization, militancy and common cause that will be capable of challenging the powers that be. It is in this spirit, and with the conviction that another world is possible and necessary, that we offer the work that lies ahead.

PART ONE

Solidarity research

ONE

The methods of movements: academic crisis and activist strategy

For the majority world – for everyone outside the walls of the enclaves of privilege located disproportionately (though by no means exclusively) in the global North – globalized neoliberal capitalism and its logic of accumulation by dispossession (Harvey 2003; McNally 2011) have been only the most recent chapter in a more than five-century history of genocide, colonialism and imperialism. In recent years, the interests of transnationalized capital have been accorded a place of pre-eminence, whether through free-trade agreements, debt and aid, 'development projects' and structural adjustment programmes, or counter-insurgency and military intervention. In the global North, within the belly of the beast, great social violence has been unleashed by neoliberalism: increasingly precarious or non-existent work, entrenched and deepening inequality and immiseration, the evisceration of public services, the enclosure of public space and the augmentation of the state's repressive apparatuses alongside the withering of its commitments to even the most basic elements of social welfare. This has meant nothing less than a low-intensity socio-economic war against actors, institutions and practices identified as contrary or marginal to this neoliberal order, notably women, queer and trans folk, people of colour, migrants, Indigenous nations and those considered disabled. If ever there was a time for robust, formidable social movements, that time is now.

Until recently, the apparent dearth of movements capable of contesting this globalized regime of elite 'accumulation by dispossession' (Harvey 2003) led many to decry the absence of a radical imagination. After all, in the face of a naked calculus that declared banks and corporations 'too big to fail' while condemning broad swathes of humanity (to say nothing of the planet or non-human life) to economic and social oblivion, it seemed self-evident that the spark necessary to animate radicalized mass movements was conspicuously absent, extinguished perhaps by neoliberalism's enclosure of the lifeworld and the privatization of all things public. If people had once 'dreamed big' and sought unapologetically to change the world, more than two decades into the 'end of history' such dreams now seemed smothered by the rampant individualism, claustrophobic cynicism and reactionary backlash engendered by neoliberal social engineering and shrill neoconservative moralism (see Haiven 2014). In 2011, this dismal landscape was fractured by the explosive emergence of the uprisings in the Arab world, the Occupy movement and the 'movement of the squares'. For many, participants and observers alike, these movements represent the rediscovery of the radical imagination, so long dormant (Graeber 2011). Of course, all these movements have confronted formidable challenges since the heady days of their emergence in 2011. Dynamics of repression, co-optation and the difficult work of sustaining movements notwithstanding, these mass manifestations of rage and hope have served to illuminate some important socio-political dynamics with respect to the terrain of social change in the age of austerity. In reclaiming public space – in a physical and communicative sense – and unabashedly refusing to capitulate to the elite invocation that there could be no alternative to the status quo, these movements have ruptured and transformed the capitalist imaginative landscape and allowed new visions of social transformation to rush into the vacuum.

Crisis

Invoked frequently since the turn of the millennium, the word 'crisis' has become so ubiquitous that it has, ironically, been rendered banal, deployed to describe a wide variety of circumstances – humanitarian, ecological, economic, political, social, moral, and so on – in need of some kind of urgent attention or intervention. Careful attention to its use nevertheless reveals a different truth. Rather than functioning as a rallying cry for collective action, it often serves to obfuscate rather than illuminate, demobilize rather than inspire. After all, crisis is by its very nature complex, massive and overwhelming, a problem of such immense proportions that it is almost unimaginable in scope. While crisis implicates us all, in the context of hierarchical, highly stratified and technocratic societies, its solutions are all too often entrusted to the powerful. Indeed, crises seem to call out for expert knowledge, specialized intervention, blueprints for action crafted by professional insiders. Of course, that's the point to crisis. Rather than challenging the status quo and setting the stage for a radical unsettling of it in order to make room for something new, the crisis trope encloses our collective imagination of what is possible, narrowing it to focus on the crisis as defined by those with the power to proclaim it. Once proclaimed and defined, crisis management becomes the banner beneath which all manner of elite projects can march and behind which the rest of us are expected to fall in line.

The elite-driven project of accumulation by dispossession that has followed in the wake of the most recent convulsions of global capitalism is a case study in these dynamics. Rather than the 2008 collapse of credit markets being seen as perhaps the result of deep systemic flaws (exacerbated by years of neo-liberal deregulation and corporate consolidation in the financial sector), the origins of the crisis were displaced onto renegade individuals: rogue traders, subprime mortgage hucksters and the subprime borrowers themselves. More importantly, an elaborate fiction was spun regarding the necessity that the vast majority of the world's population diminish their expectations, commit to generations of precarity, abandon the hope for societies which publicly and collectively provide for the needs of those who constitute them, and embrace a vastly augmented security state along with entrenched and deepening inequality. The solution to the crisis was then christened 'austerity', in whose holy name a historically unprecedented transfer of public wealth into private hands is occurring, allegedly to ameliorate this crisis (Blythe 2013).

We can add to this the way that the present economic crisis and the crisis of austerity are fundamentally built upon and contribute to the racialized and gendered patterns of exploitation, oppression and inequality that are the bedrock of the capitalist system. As the economic and social crises deepen, the costs are disproportionately borne by women, people of colour, migrant workers and others whose subjugation has always been central to accumulation. As austerity regimes dismantle what remains of the welfare state, poverty deepens and efforts to redress historical inequalities are abandoned. As social programmes are slashed, the 'reproductive' labour once offered through state schools, health-care systems and pensions is downloaded to individuals and families, typically to women.

The worsening crisis leads to new waves of un- and under-employment, to greater stress and anxiety, to greater alienation, and with these we see the resurgence of religious fundamentalisms, ethnic nationalism, violent xenophobia and racist backlash that target society's most vulnerable and marginalized. While recent years have seen important victories for feminist, queer, trans and other movements, there is no end to oppression, though sometimes it emerges in subtler forms. But as the crisis wreaks havoc on the pillars of conventional masculinity (the ability to have meaningful work and support a family, etc.) we see the rebirth of far-right and regressive male anger directed towards these groups. Meanwhile, a culture of individualistic competition misinterprets the crisis as resulting from the 'greed' of 'special interest groups' (including unions, civil rights and multicultural organizations, the arts, etc.) and fosters a vindictive politics of punitive cuts, surveillance and loathing. All this permits and enables the displacing of the crisis of capitalism onto the social realm, making the systemic crisis of accumulation a general crisis of social reproduction.

None of this is to suggest the existence of some secret cabal engaged in crafting an elaborate conspiracy; nor do we imagine the bulk of society either as mystified masses in the thrall of elites or without agency and thus entirely absolved of complicity in perpetuating systemic inequality, exploitation and violence. But recognizing this complexity should not mean retreating into some muddy realm of complete relativity where everyone can be understood as equally victim and victimizer. A system of exploitation and violence may dehumanize the oppressor, but this in no way should be seen as equivalent to costs borne by those oppressed within such systems. There is a profound inequality in terms of who reaps the rewards of participating in and perpetuating such systems.

Research, enclosure and academic capital

Of course, crisis is nothing new to the academy, post-secondary education, research or scholarship. While crises of various kinds have been the object of study for many academics, crisis has increasingly come to define the state of many disciplines and of the university itself. With the rise of neoliberal capitalism in the 1970s and a vicious neoconservative moral order in the 1980s, a wide variety of practices and institutions associated with the liberal welfare state and the class compromise it brokered became prime targets for elites eager to build a new world order premised on unfettered corporate profiteering enforced by repressive and juridical state apparatuses (Harvey 2005). Neoliberal capitalism emerged in the 1970s as a response to 'the contradictions between democratically governed national states responsive at least partially to citizens' needs and a global economy organized around profit-seeking [transnational corporations] and increasingly stateless financial capital' (Carroll and Ratner 2005: 11). Indeed, in 1975, the Trilateral Commission

— an unelected and unaccountable coterie of elites representing Europe, North America and Japan, brought together to foster inter-elite 'dialogue' and 'cooperation' on political and economic issues — wrung its collective hands over what it perceived as 'an excess of democracy' generating 'a breakdown of traditional means of social control, a delegitimation of political and other forms of authority, and an overload of demands on government, exceeding its capacity to respond' (Crozier et al. 1975: 8). From this perspective, the problem seemed to be that while capital accumulation was entirely the province of elites, the trappings of liberal democracy still allowed the rest of society to evade total domination. While Keynesian social welfarism had sought to dull somewhat the cutting edges of capitalism by ameliorating some of its worst consequences through state programmes and intervention — in order, it should be understood, not to subvert it but to ensure its survival in the face of explicitly radical and revolutionary challenges — neoliberalism celebrates and proliferates social division and inequality as a mechanism for furthering the capitalist domination of society, effectively addressing the vexatious issues raised by the Trilateral Commission and others. In this way, rather than signalling the decline of the state as an apparatus of control, neoliberalism actually increases the need for a 'well-armoured' one (Carroll and Ratner 2005: 12). Indeed, as Wendy Brown (2010) notes, the decline of state sovereignty in the economic realm has led to a desperate attempt to exert punitive authority over social life, especially by targeting marginalized groups, migrants, refugees and other alleged 'outsiders'.

The consequences of neoliberalism, however, reach far beyond the material realm. As cultural theorist Henry Giroux (2004) has argued, neoliberalism represents nothing less than the subordina-tion of the lifeworld by capital: the enclosure of that which was common, the privatization of that which was public, and an overarching policy of militarization and surveillance aimed at ensuring the compliance of the ruled. The implications of this privatization of the social commons by capital has implications for critical inquiry, scholarship and the university.

Indeed, the university has become a key site of struggle both in terms of what it could offer to capital (research and development, resources, expertise) and what it might do as a space – however imperfect – of critical and free inquiry. Within the university, the social engineering neoliberalism has sought to achieve more broadly has been replicated. Disciplines that can offer something substantial to the interests of capital (engineering, applied sciences, business) have been celebrated while those seen as marginal or opposed to them (many of the humanities and social sciences) have been maligned and defunded. For those disciplines that do not immediately present themselves as instrumentally useful to a new regime of capital accumulation, survival becomes predicated on the capacity to make a case for (and, in many cases, remake themselves in order to achieve) their relevance to labour markets and the potential for corporate partnerships (Martin 2011; Bousquet 2008; Edu-factory Collective 2009). This is not a lament for the bygone days of the liberal university, imagined as a place of free inquiry, democratic participation and critical discussion. Such a place has never existed. Indeed, we would do well to remember that dominant institutions like the university have always been tied to the production and reproduction of the social order in which they are enmeshed (Wallerstein 1996).

Here the insights of the transnational Edu-factory Collective (2009; Roggero 2011) are particularly instructive. Under the maxim 'as once the factory, so now the university', they draw attention to three ways academe has become a key institution of global power and contestation. First, the idea of the 'edu-factory' alerts us to the 'industrialized' character of education in an age of its commodification, when university degrees are seen as purchasable credentials and where budget cuts, the calcification of disciplines, and institutional restructuring increasingly cast education as a standardized product rather than a reflexive process of personal and social transformation. At their worst, universities have become dynamos of a nightmare version of what critical pedagogy scholar Paolo Freire (2000) has called the 'banking model' of education: one where prepackaged knowledge is deposited in discrete chunks into students' heads to be stored for later withdrawal, at testing time or in the workplace.

Second, it alerts us to the way the university today, like the factory of the industrial age, acts as a key laboratory for developing new ways to discipline labour. On the one hand, not only do students emerge from universities with an education increasingly oriented towards 'job-ready skills'; they also typically graduate heavily indebted, and that debt acts as a form of labour discipline when they enter the workplace, diminishing their capacity for resistance and refusal by creating the omnipresent fear that unemployment will lead to financial ruin (see Caffentzis 2013; Williams 2008). On the other hand, the university is also the scene of new techniques for harnessing the energy, enthusiasm and aspirations of its increasingly precarious employees. The overproduction of Ph.D.s and the glut of hopeful university teachers means that, to a greater and greater extent, the university relies on a massive 'reserve army' of underemployed would-be academics working from contract to contract with few guarantees (Bousquet 2008). Yet this is quickly becoming the norm even beyond the university, as precarious work based on the (self-)exploitation of workers' hopes and dreams that they may one day be able to 'do what they love' becomes the expected norm in many sectors of the economy. The university, as the Edu-factory Collective argue, has become a model for the proletarianization of cognitive labour more generally.

Finally, the idea of the edu-factory draws our attention to the fact that a huge proportion of the population in the global North now passes through university, rendering it an acute site of struggle. In the industrial age, the factory represented the fulcrum of society, the institution on which society pivoted. This made it a powerful focus for social movement organizing. Today, while the university remains in many ways a highly privileged and elitist place, it is also one institution that increasingly dominates the landscape of work and life, even if its impact is limited to the way it excludes some individuals from access and, hence, the material and social privileges that allegedly accompany a university degree. In many post-industrial cities, the university sector is the largest single employer; integration into the pharmaceuticals, security, weapons, finance and medical sectors has seen expansion of the university's scope and influence. Numerically speaking, more people may today pass through the doors of a university (as students, as workers, as contractees, etc.) than ever passed through the gates of a factory in years gone by.

To be clear, the Edu-factory Collective is not suggesting that factories have ceased to be key sites of struggle and exploitation, though largely production has been moved outside the global North to locales where labour is cheaper and more readily exploitable. Nor are they likening the plight of the student or the precarious academic worker to the back-breaking and soul-crushing labours of industrial workers or their families. But they do want to alert us to the fact that, more than simply navel-gazing, the politics of the university *matter* in an age of 'cognitive capitalism', when increasingly capital is interested not only in harnessing our labour time to create commodities to sell to generate surplus value (as per the traditional Marxist model), but also in commodifying and privatizing social life, and transforming the society itself into a 'factory' for the reproduction of capitalist social relations (see Hardt and Virno 1996).

Edu-factory's approach owes its theoretical and political orientation to what has come to be known as 'autonomist Marxism', a school of thought and action associated with the *autonomia* and *post-oparaismo* movements in Italy in the 1970s (see Wright 2002). A key dimension of these radical movements, which rejected mainstream political participation in favour of building militant solidarity and autonomy among workers and students at the grassroots, was the practice of 'workers enquiry'. This refers to a set of approaches or a methodological strategy of insurgent, bottom-up sociology and 'co-research' which was developed by autonomist thinkers and organizers based on a rejection of the top-down, doctrinaire models provided by academia or the established communist and socialist parties of the day. Instead of taking a bird's-eye view of the rapid industrialization of Northern Italian cities in the 1970s and seeking to apply prepackaged Marxist frameworks, these researchers sought to study the everyday dynamics of power and resistance in workplaces, and to do so through discussion groups, one-on-one biographical interviews, and reading groups with workers themselves.

The paradigm of workers' enquiry or 'co-research' has expanded and spread beyond Italy in the intervening years (see Shukaitis, Graeber, and Biddle 2007) to encompass research with social movements and in other social spheres in ways that pay close and earnest attention to the particularities of circumstance, without losing sight of the broader systems of power in which they are enmeshed. Critically, this tradition sees research as a collaborative venture aimed at empowering workers' communities and seeks to make the gulf between theory and action a tangible and workable problem to be solved in practice. We consider our own Radical Imagination Project as inspired in part by this tradition. For the Edu-factory Collective, beginning with objective and subjective conditions of oppression, exploitation, depression, exasperation, consternation and anger within the university is key to understanding an institution that might otherwise appear to an orthodox Marxist critic as a bastion of bourgeois privilege. It also opens the door to the potential of research and study to be transformative acts (see Harney and Moten 2013).

The issue at hand has nothing to do with a return to an imagined ivory tower that never was. Rather, it is entirely about how institutions like the university, and scholars at work within the matrices of power they enclose, function either to facilitate the construction of more just, democratic, egalitarian and liberated socio-political and economic orders, or to entrench, defend and deepen power, privilege and inequality (see Chapters 7 and 8). This book explores what engaged research might offer to struggles for social change and the construction of a more just, democratic, dignified, liberated and peaceful world. At stake is a concept of common research that sees beyond the limits of the present and also the disciplinary and institutional boundaries of the current order. Such an approach would see research as more than just the production of disciplinary knowledge for the accumulation of 'academic capital', the ways in which academic production can constitute a form of what Pierre Bourdieu (1984) calls symbolic capital, and the way, in turn, that symbolic capital has real material implications (positions, salaries, research funds, etc.). Such an approach would see beyond the pieties the surround the allegedly inherent nobility of the academic search for truth. Rather, it would (radically) imagine research as part of an evolving social process, and imagine the researcher less as a collector of data and a generator of discrete articles of knowledge and more as a convener or convoker of social processes within and beyond academe (see Wilson 2009). If the university has always been (in different ways) an institution of capitalism and colonialism, and if research is its legitimation and its product, what would 'research' look like in a post-capitalist society? And how might a vision of this inform and shape the research activities in our present day?

Social movement scholarship and the politics of knowledge production

The history of scholarly attempts to make sense of social movement activity is an archive of the politics of knowledge production and the interests such intellectual labour has served. Prior to the 1960s, collective behaviour theory was the dominant scholarly perspective on social movement activity. From an unabashedly functionalist perspective, collective behaviour theory cast social movements as little more than instances of mob behaviour, 'escape valves' for the supposedly unarticulated and misdirected frustrations of the lower classes and social malcontents with no real bearing upon politics as such. For the collective behaviourists, movements, at best, served as forms of collective catharsis maintaining the equilibrium of the system as a whole (see Staggenborg 2012: 13–14). Such a perspective is hardly surprising, given that throughout this period universities were unapologetically elitist institutions, staffed typically by conservative scholars dedicated to perpetuating the status quo. From their perspective, social movement activity was pathological.

The dramatic upsurge on a global scale in social movement activity in the 1960s cast serious doubt on the assumptions animating the functionalist paradigm. This was so because many of these movements – feminist, queer, civil rights, anti-war, anti-colonial, anti-imperialist, student, Black and Red Power – could not be easily reconciled with the mob caricature due to their intentionality and organization in addition to the eloquent and powerful critiques and alternatives they advanced to the status quo and the vested interests at work within it (see Edelman 2001; Katsiaficas 1987). Rather than seeking representation within existing institutions, which they perceived as built to serve the vested interests of elites, many of these movements took aim at the systems they saw as responsible for perpetuating inequality, exploitation and violence, and contested the very way in which social life was constituted and organized.

Our own use of the term 'radical' belongs to this legacy of movements and approaches that understand the problems confronting them as irresolvable within the structure of the current political system and so seek systemic change rather than piecemeal reform (see Day 2005; Holloway 2002). With the crumbling of collective behaviour theory's mindless mob narrative in the face of the rise of the New Left in the 1960s, North American sociologists advanced political process and resource mobilization models, at least in part as a way to conceptualize social movements as genuinely political actors rather than aberrant psychological phenomena (Staggenborg 2012: 18). At the same time, in Europe social movement scholars were elaborating what would become known as new social movement (NSM) theory (see Melucci 1985; Touraine 2002). While both these schools of social movement analysis represented significant breaks with the preceding functionalist perspective, they also advanced divergent conceptualizations of social movements and their activity (see Tarrow 1988). These advances in social movement scholarship were enabled and mirrored by a transformation within the university. What had once been an elitist institution was, in the wake of the Second World War, being transformed into a public, mass institution, seen as central to economic development and social cohesion in an increasingly knowledge-driven world. As such, a wider variety of students and (to a lesser extent) faculty found themselves in the university system, and with them new perspectives on social contestation. The expansion of the welfare state in the post-war period also saw greater opportunities for the social sciences and more room for the development of methodological and theoretical paradigms. And, more generally, the coming-of-age of the Baby-Boom generation saw campuses ignite as spaces of struggle and experimentation.

From the political process/resource mobilization perspective, movements were viewed as collective political actors making claims against the dominant order whose success depended largely upon their capacity to mobilize resources, material (organizational infrastructure, funding, etc.) and immaterial (leadership, member commitment, social capital, etc.). It also sought to contextualize movements within the political system itself (the presence or absence of institutional allies or challengers, the relative openness of the system, the system's perceived legitimacy). While the political process/resource mobilization paradigm represented a significant advance over collective behaviour theory in terms of the robustness of its analysis and its willingness to take movements seriously as legitimate political actors, the paradigm still fundamentally located movements – however radical or militant – as merely one political player among others seeking to leverage influence and affect change within the established socio-political and economic order and largely in the terms set by that order.

Across the Atlantic, European scholars were elaborating a school of social movement inquiry that would become known as NSM theory, which advanced a perspective that focused on macro-social struggles, seeing movements originating in the 1960s and after as engaged in post-material struggles revolving around issues relating to the nature and constitution of social life itself in the context of late or 'post-industrial' capitalism (see Melucci 1985; Touraine 2002). According to NSM theory, while 'old' social movements (like organized labour) fought for material benefits, 'new' social movements (like the anti-nuclear and peace movements) concerned themselves with the deep logic of the social order, contesting not only the material consequences of a system governed by inequality but the very structure of the system itself. While the NSM paradigm contributed significantly to scholarly understandings of social movements in ways that exceeded the functionalism of collective behaviour and the liberalist framework of political process/resource mobilization theory, it was by no means free of shortcomings. In focusing so prominently on distinguishing 'new' from 'old' social movements the NSM paradigm posited a radical break in forms of collective contentious action that obscured important continuities. In emphasizing 'immaterial' struggles over the social logics of 'post-industrial' capitalist society, the NSM perspective also tended to ignore the structural nature of violence, oppression and exploitation, and valorized struggles that in the main belonged to more privileged social actors and classes.

Of course, none of this is to suggest that dominant social movement studies paradigms have not yielded valuable insights for understanding the dynamics of social change and contentious action. Such work has even, at times, served to legitimate social movement activity in the eyes of the mainstream as genuinely political and not merely aberrant or pathological. Sometimes this research has been driven by the values of solidarity, and has occasionally seen researchers work with or for movements. Some of the shortcomings present in earlier paradigms have also been corrected, with a more recent focus by social movement scholars on issues including emotion and biography (Goodwin, Jasper and Polletta 2001; Jasper 1999), consciousness (Mansbridge and Morris

2001), issue framing (Benford and Snow 1992; Olesen 2005), networks (Keck and Sikkink 1998), and globalization and transnationalism (Bandy and Smith 2005; Della Porta, Kriesi and Rucht 2009). Nevertheless, since its inception, the field of social movement studies has tended to approach social movements as 'objects' of study in a manner not dissimilar to an engineer studying a closed hydraulic system. In many cases, the analysis and its significance remain functionalist in spirit even if the substance of the analysis has moved away from such restrictions. In this sense, the form of analysis and its expression betray the epistemological and ontological assumptions of the researcher and the norms of the field (see Lal 2002). When the 'objects' under consideration deviate radically from these norms, the stakes and consequences of such disciplined interpretations increase considerably. For example, it is one thing to use conventional liberal paradigms to analyse mobilizations and campaigns occurring under the banner of 'Make Poverty History' – a campaign closely tied to the UN Millennium Development Goals and linked to organized labour, faith groups and the NGO development sector. It is quite another to try to use the same analytical schema to explore radical anti-capitalist organizing on a transnational scale as it unfolded under the auspices of networks like People's Global Action at the height of the alter-globalization movement, which were decentralized, based on the principle of local autonomy and characterized by an anarchistic commensurability of means and ends (see Day 2005; Graeber 2009; Juris 2008; Maeckelbergh 2009; Wood 2012).

The expansion of more nuanced and thoughtful approaches to social movement studies may be symptomatic of another shift in the university. Whereas the period of the New Left was marked by the vast expansion of academe and its transformation from an elite to a public institution (though one that never fully relinquished its elitism), the period of neoliberalism and today's social movements has, as we have discussed, seen the fragmentation, privatization and commodification of the university and the rise of an increasingly precarious, competitive and productivity-oriented form of academic labour. On the one hand, such a transformation has fundamentally shrunk the space and time available for solidarity-based research and activism within the university. Yet it has also led to the hyper-production (perhaps overproduction) of academic writing on social movements and social-justice-related themes. While such a proliferation is, in part, evidence of the desperate need for would-be scholars to 'publish or perish' and generate the academic capital necessary to leverage secure university employment, it has also opened up a plurality of new avenues for inquiry and theorization.

Yet, in spite of good intentions, social movement scholars have often misrepresented and domesticated social movements by trying to explain them in the dominant academic paradigm, or in ways that seek to normalize them within the existing landscape of socio-political relations. As Marina Sitrin argues, a focus on 'contentious politics', so common among North American social movement scholars, renders all movements 'in a contentious relationship to the state, or another form or institution with formal "power over," whether demanding reforms from or desiring another state or institution' (2012: 13). But the radical challenge issued by some movements to the status quo, as well as the imaginations, hopes and desires inspiring them, are often lost in such a framing. When we merely seek to contextualize social movements in terms of the demands they make on (or responses they have to) the dominant socio-political order, we fail to understand that social movements are, both explicitly and implicitly, challenging that order and actively seeking to imagine and create alternatives. If we miss this key dimension of social movement activity (even among seemingly liberal or reformist movements), we fail to grasp some of their most salient and important features. It is for this reason that we need to take a broader perspective if we are to truly understand the radical imagination, and strive to devise methods based on the principles of solidarity.

Social movements, stories and ethnography

In his work on the importance of story to revolutionary movements and moments, social movement scholar Eric Selbin argues that it is through the collective telling and retelling of stories that the possibility of resistance, rebellion and revolution persists. Selbin contends that such a recognition necessitates 'a systematic return of stories to social science methodology', a move that acknowledges and is capable of engaging 'the myth and memory of revolution and of the power of mimesis for the mobilization and sustenance of revolutionary activity' (2010: 3–4). Selbin's contention is not simply that stories matter but that, when considered comprehensively, their telling and retelling constitute 'a story structure, a repository of stories which undergirds and shapes our daily lives' (2010: 45). He goes further:

> We (re)compose stories and (re)configure them in an effort to (re)connect with each other and to build community.... Truth, direct or otherwise, is less important than the extent to which stories represent people's perceptions or capture what they feel. They form a collection of who we were and where we came from, where and who we are now, and guide us to where we are going and who we wish to be. (Selbin 2010: 46)

Selbin focuses on four key types of revolutionary story in his work, but the way he articulates the importance of story to social change struggles has much broader implications as well. In social movement studies, 'diffusion' is the catch-all term used to signify the circulation of ideas about and repertoires of contentious action through movements and the activists who constitute them (see Tarrow 2005; Wood 2012). Such examinations primarily consider the mechanisms (ideal relations between actors, communications technologies, media, training sessions) facilitating diffusion while attending somewhat to the significance of context in facilitating or inhibiting diffusion. Why these ideas and repertoires of struggle *matter* – what they signify and how they work to construct collective visions of political possibility that animate struggle – is accorded much less significance. The application of framing theory to explain how movements engage in meaning-making and symbolic contestation has similarly yielded results that are analytically sophisticated, but that rarely probe beyond the mechanisms (human rights discourses, digital media, the Internet, etc.) facilitating such struggles (see Olesen 2005).

A much more embodied, robust and engaged perspective on social movements – particularly the newest ones emerging out of and in the wake of the alter-globalization movement – has been advanced by a constellation of explicitly politicized social science researchers. Work by David Graeber (2007; 2009), Jeffrey Juris (2008), Juris and Khasnabish (2013) Alex Khasnabish (2008), Marianne Maeckelbergh (2009), Marina Sitrin (2012), the Turbulence Collective (2010) and Lesley Wood (2012), for example, exhibits a strong tendency not only to engage with movements on the ground and from an avowedly politicized stance but to take movements seriously as fecund ecologies rife with possibility. Many of these works, though by no means all, are ethnographic in their form and methodology, an important departure from the core of social movement studies that has tended to privilege structural, institutional and organizational perspectives. Without simplistically elevating ethnographic methods, it is worth ruminating upon what ethnographically grounded approaches to social movement research can provide in contrast to conventional social movements studies perspectives. In order to do so it is necessary to unpack 'ethnography'.

Ethnography needs to be understood not only as a genre of scholarly writing characterized by 'thick description', or even as a set of research methods grounded in participant observation and immersion in 'the field', but as a perspective committed to understanding and taking seriously people's lived realities. As such, rather than using movements as objects of analysis from which to abstract general theories of contentious action and social change, ethnographic approaches dwell in the terrain of 'immanence': the lived realities which constitute the fabric of social movement activity and existence. Ethnographic methods including participant observation, long-term fieldwork and in-depth interviews are founded on the conviction that the world does not simply comprise objects to be analysed but is acted and imagined into being by active, dialogic subjects, including researchers themselves. Because of its groundedness and its willingness to take matters of subjectivity seriously, ethnography is a research posture particularly well suited to exploring dynamic phenomena such as social movements in their less tangible dimensions. Ethnography is also a perspective and methodology that lends itself well to engaged research that is committed to taking part in, rather than merely observing, struggles for social change. Anarchist and anthropologist David Graeber has gone so far as to suggest that ethnography could be a model for the 'would-be non-vanguardist revolutionary intellectual' because it offers the possibility 'of teasing out the tacit logic or principles underlying certain forms of radical practice, and then, not only offering the analysis back to those communities, but using them to formulate new visions' (2007: 310). Jeffrey Juris has articulated a similar vision of 'militant' ethnographic practice which refuses the valorization of 'objective distance' and the tendency within the academy to treat social life as an object to decode (2008: 20). Juris contends that in order '[t]o grasp the concrete logic generating specific practices, one has to become an active participant' and within the context of social movements this means participating in and contributing to the work of these movements themselves (2008: 20). As an example of this, in bringing together a variety of ethnographers with direct experience with various manifestations of the Occupy movement, Juris and Razsa (2012) note provocatively that 'activist anthropologists' might be considered the 'organic intellectuals' of the Occupy movement, given the roles played by many within the movement, roles that were complementary to, rather than outside of, their research commitments.

Again, without unduly valorizing ethnography, the interventions made by engaged ethnographers in the study of social
movements, particularly in their more radical manifestations,
point towards what methodological choices and practices can
illuminate and what they obscure. At issue is not simply the
question of subjective versus objective knowledge but of how
we understand the nature of struggles for social change and the
scholarly 'vocation' itself (Khasnabish and Haiven 2012). Central
here is how we conceive of movement success and failure, and,
reflexively, how we imagine the success and failure of research
itself, a set of questions we examine in more detail in Chapter
4. If, for example, we look at social movements through the
lens of hegemonic mainstream social movement studies, we see
movements as organizations whose principal objective is policy
change, which they seek to achieve through pressure leveraged
against dominant political institutions and actors. Success is
measured by a movement's ability to achieve this end and to
sustain itself. Of course, what disappears from view through
this lens are the multiple effects produced by movements that
are non-institutional and non-instrumental in nature and that
are not necessarily limited to the lifespan of a given movement
but that may be understood only when positioned against a
much longer arc of networked struggle. For example, absent
from this conceptualization and analysis are the effects produced
by movements that have contested racism, misogyny, capitalism
and war, the struggles of which successfully challenged the
relations and ideologies sustaining these structural forms of
violence at the level of everyday social reality but which never
achieved or articulated a desire to change specific policies and
practices. Of critical importance to this attentive perspective

is an understanding of social movements not as 'things' but as products of the collective labour and imagination of those who constitute them. Attending to movements as the outcomes of the relations that constitute them leads the analytical eye away from their most superficial effects like policy change or electoral impacts, and instead foregrounds struggle as a product of collective encounters between activists, organizers, allies, opponents and the broader public.

David Featherstone's (2012) work on solidarity as a transformative political relationship rather than a 'thing' to be achieved (or not) demonstrates the utility of this approach. Tracing histories and geographies of left internationalism, Featherstone excavates the labour of building solidarity between different actors engaged in a multitude of different struggles, a process that is never devoid of conflict, power relations or inequality but that, when successful, has the ability to reshape the field of political possibility as well as to transform the subjectivity of those engaged. A critical focus on the relationality at the heart of radical movements has also been a focus of ethnographically grounded engaged social movement scholarship (see Graeber 2009; Juris 2008; Juris and Khasnabish 2013; Khasnabish 2008; Maeckelbergh 2009; Sitrin 2012). Instead of focusing on instrumental outcomes of movements, and reading success and failure through a lens focusing on institutional impact, these works insist on the significance of understanding and engaging movements as living spaces of encounter, possibility, contestation and conflict. As Sitrin contends in her work on horizontalism and autonomy in the newest social movements in Argentina, 'participants speak of the success of the movements, and of a success that is not measurable by traditional social science, but rather one that is measured by the formation and continuation of new social relationships, new subjectivities, and a new-found dignity' (2012: 14). Such movements do not merely serve as vehicles for the dissemination of 'action repertoires'; they are laboratories for experimenting with ways of imagining and living otherwise (see McKay 2005).

There are a few central virtues of ethnography for our purposes. Primarily, it liberates us from more positivistic and scientistic methods that imagine social movements as self-contained billiard balls ricocheting around the political table, merely one political or sociological actor among many. Rather, ethnography reveals the deeply dialogic, incomplete and innovative nature of social movements. It encourages us to attend to the way movements are formed by circumstances, relationships, possibilities, personalities, dreams, identities and, importantly, the imagination. It facilitates our exploration of the ways social movements, in turn, help reshape all these things, both among their participants and in society at large. In a world (and a university) obsessed with reducing complexities to utile (often, but not exclusively, quantitative) units of knowledge, ethnography gives us the courage to dwell in messiness, in the rats' nest of interconnectivity. Ethnographic methods allow us to see *how* social movements are nothing more, but also nothing less, than creators of history, not merely bit players in the drama of social elites.

Second, ethnography allows us to displace and problematize the locus of knowledge production. Rather than seeing the researcher as a figure who produces knowledge *about* the world, ethnography at its best sees the researcher more as a translator or storyteller. The militant ethnographer brings the rigours of academe to social movements and seeks to find ways that theoretical, methodological and conceptual approaches might be useful to movements. They also bring the wisdom, creativity and thoughtfulness of social movements 'back' to other publics, for better or for worse. Ethnography can, at best, suggest a radical humility, one we think appropriate to the crisis of the edu-factory. Such an approach seeks to self-consciously avoid research as an act of enclosure, instead seeing it as a way of creating and sustaining new commons.

The vocation of research

These attempts to take movements and their activities seriously raise questions of what social movement scholarship is good for. At stake here is what we would frame as the question of solidarity. If research is to be about more than generating academic capital, it must in some way serve the interests of those whom it claims to value. Yet if research is to be more than participation, it must also at some point offer something rigorous, candid and theoretically informed. In other words, solidarity research requires some degree of strategy to manage or navigate competing interests and the inherent tension between the (good and bad) demands of social movements and the (good and bad) demands of the university.

In a reductionist way, we have characterized two broad solidarity research *strategies* within the current idiom. We have characterized these approaches (and our own third strategy) with reference to the idea of 'voice' as charted by Nick Couldry (2010), for whom the ability to articulate a critical voice in public is both what neoliberal capitalism has confiscated from us and that talent which the university must struggle to rekindle. This notion of 'voice' resonates with the idea of a 'vocation' or a 'calling', a term frequently used to describe the motive of the academic researcher. With its connotations of religious piety and self-sacrifice, the idea of research as a 'vocation' can lead us to adopt the mythology of the exploitative university, which holds that researchers are an inherently benevolent, aloof and paternalistic clergy who produce objective knowledge that is ultimately in the public interest (even if the 'public' in question is imagined to be too stupid to understand how and why). We reject this connotation, and instead adopt the notion of 'vocation': being called to a voice. We see the researcher less as a chaste and sacrosanct monk and more as someone who has dedicated themselves to giving voice to those dimensions of life that all too often remain unspoken. At its best, the research breaks those sedimented silences of history and interrupts the monotonous normative reproduction of social life and its accumulated injustices. Yet how to do this valuable work is a difficult matter of strategy, especially when it comes to solidarity research.

On the one hand, there is the call of a relatively traditional methodological vocation. Those adopting this approach have tended to suggest either that the values of avowedly empiricist research methods are consonant with social movement aims (the pursuit of truth and knowledge against the forces of falsity and ignorance, the dispassionate revelation of the injustices of the world, or the sanctity of the university as a critical but detached social institution) or that more traditional inquiry into social movements offers those movements validation and legitimacy within the university and in society more broadly. While this strategy is associated with many different research methods (qualitative and quantitative, policy-oriented or ethnographic) we might call this a 'strategy of invocation' because its political efficacy stems from the iterative power of the academic and their invoking of social movements as legitimate and important sites of social intercourse and creativity. This strategy seeks to give voice to social movements, mobilizing the privilege, esteem and social location of the university to articulate and amplify movements.

On the other hand, there is a calling away from these more traditional approaches and towards a vocation that puts scholarly skills directly at the disposal of social movements themselves. Highlighting the ways movements create, critique and teach their own forms of critical knowledge (in many cases, much more successfully than the university, at least by social movement standards) researchers in this vein stress methods that take direction from and integrate themselves within the struggles of social movements, especially when they are centred around constituencies typically marginalized in society and (rightly) distrustful of academic inquiry.

This strategy, largely inspired by and growing out of feminist action research (see Farrow, Moss and Shaw 1995; Harding 2004; Hesse-Biber 2012; Maguire 1996), has mobilized a wide diversity of methods, from conducting surveys of movement and community participants to writing policy alternatives with social movements, to seeing researchers drop all pretence of producing 'knowledge' and instead 'getting their hands dirty' in organizing or even taking up arms. We call this a 'strategy of avocation', a calling-away-from, to signal the difficulty of working between vocations, and 'called away' by both social movement solidarity and academic work, of being torn. Those practising this strategy astutely note the power and privilege academic researchers wield and many have done the slow, difficult and often painful work of building trust and solidarity with social movements and developing a reflexive, critical accounting for their participation. They must also often undertake the heartbreaking work of justifying their scholarly work to unfriendly academic colleagues and administrators obsessed with 'peer'-reviewed research 'outputs' and distrustful of work that, by its very nature, calls attention to the fact that all research is political (see Hess-Biber 2012).

Both of these broad strategies have, at times, been extremely successful in terms of serving social movements and of producing valuable academic text, and it is not our desire to level a criticism at either. Our objective is to consider another strategy. We are led to do so by some hard thinking about the particular location and responsibility of university-based social research in neoliberal times, as well as the current state of social movements with regard to the radical imagination. Our experiment begins with a question: what are the unique features of our own subject locations as university researchers that would allow us to make a *meaningful* and *unique* contribution both to social movements in our locality and to our academic community? Can we imagine and experiment with a *strategy* of social movement research that (1) strives for a recognition of the specificities of the social location, privilege, constraint, and power of researchers; (2) mobilizes or leverages this situatedness to provide social movements with a *space* or a *time* that they cannot or do not provide for themselves; and (3) continues to contribute to radical academic scholarly dialogue?

For us, the strategy of invocation is insufficient, although we have both practised such a strategy in the past. We feel

that merely reporting on and affirming social movement activity does not answer the deepening and widening crisis we
now face. The ways in which such a strategy contributes to
social movement struggle are not direct enough. While we
may use our academic work to point out promising new
developments in social movements, or the way they 'prefigure'
a better future, who really is paying attention? Certainly not
most social movements, which find our scholarly publications
inaccessible or simply don't have time to engage with them.
Indeed, in an era of academic hyper-production, most of our
colleagues don't even have the time to read our work! Similarly, while our more dispassionate and distanced research on
social movements may offer us useful pedagogical tools with
which to attempt to radicalize our students, does this justify
yet another study of social movement X or Y? Do such projects risk offering up knowledge to forces hostile to the movements under study, such as conservative politicians, the police
or marketers eager to grasp onto images and spectacles of
authenticity? Finally, if we leverage our privilege as academics
to valorize social movements, do we not risk reaffirming our
privilege as guardians of the knowledge factory? And who, in
the end, is the real beneficiary? In short, while the strategy has
produced important, influential and inspiring work, it all too
often relies on outmoded liberal notions of the purpose of the
university and the sometimes arrogant assumption that social
movement actors and the general public should automatically
recognize the value of independent scholarly research.

On the other hand, a strategy of avocation, deep work
within movements, while incredibly valuable, does not answer
all the challenges we have laid out. Scholars who have chosen

this path have done invaluable work challenging the hubris of the academy and working with specific social movements to chart new paths for responsible and ethical social research. They also often provide key resources to those movements. But in some ways we felt this approach can cede too much of the unjust autonomy of the academic. To be clear, we are not befuddled by the myths of the university as the resplendent ivory tower whose autonomy is a sacrosanct good that can never be challenged. By autonomy here we mean a critical element of 'play' within the network of social power relations, a limited and always tenuous degree of wriggle room within the neoliberal confiscation of all things public or common. Making a fetish of our odd (almost perverse) freedom (where we are lucky enough to retain it) is unacceptable, but abandoning it is irresponsible. By folding ourselves completely within social movements, we risk losing this problematic yet productive space to create something different. More practically, our particular circumstances – which we discuss in more detail in the next chapter – were such that the social movements we are working with have not yet cohered to the point of being *able* to realistically host scholars and maintain their own autonomy. While well-established and highly organized movements may be able to imagine a constructive role for scholars in their midst, our situation was one of extreme fragmentation and, in the eyes of our research participants, inertia and fragility among social movements.

In other words, perhaps like all cases, location and situation have a hand in determining what sorts of research strategies are most apt. Hence our desire to find a different strategy, one inspired by both the strategy of invocation and the strategy of avocation but which meditates on and experiments with the particular social relations among and between social movements and social researchers in our time, in our space. It is instigated by the general agreement among both our academic and our activist colleagues that what seems to be lacking today, in social movements and in society at large, is the radical imagination: the ability to envision and work towards better futures based on an analysis of the root causes of social problems.

Convoking the radical imagination and the politics of prefiguration

Rather than focusing on analysing movements as if they were insects pinned within a shadowbox, in the Radical Imagination Project we have sought to participate in 'convoking' the radical imagination in collaboration with activists in Halifax, Nova Scotia. We sought to provide the opportunities, resources, time and space necessary to collectively bring into being the prefigurative capacity to envision and work towards building better worlds. From its earliest planning stages, we conceived of the project as an explicit attempt to 'convoke' the radical imagination − that is, to call something which is not yet fully present into being − in collaboration with activists self-identifying as 'radical' in Halifax. From the perspective of our project, the term 'radical' names movements or approaches that understand the social problems that concern them to be irresolvable within the current political system and so seek systemic change. In particular, both as researchers and as political actors, we are interested in radical social movements that have emerged in the wake of the so-called 'anti-globalization movement' and that stress values of participatory democracy, radical equality and anti-oppression towards social, economic and ecological justice (Day 2005; Juris 2008; Khasnabish 2008; Maeckelbergh 2009; Sitrin 2012; Wood 2012). As for the radical imagination – the capacity to project how the world might be otherwise – following critics like Robin Kelley (2002), Jeannette Armstrong and Douglas Cardinal (1991), and Marcel Stoetzler and Nira Yuval-Davis (2002), we have argued (Haiven and Khasnabish 2010; Khasnabish and Haiven 2012) that the imagination is a collective *process* rather than an individualized *thing*, and that its wellspring is not individual romantic geniuses but communities and collectivities as they work their way through the world.

As we discussed earlier, the term 'radical imagination' helps us frame the way radical social movements and those who constitute them seek to refashion the space of the political itself by stressing radical notions of democracy, responsibility and participation (Day 2005; Solnit 2004). Historian Ian McKay (2005) has called such radical political initiatives 'experiments in living otherwise' – social laboratories for the generation of alternative relationships, subjectivities, institutions and practices that prefigure the world these movements seek to build (see also Conway 2004). 'Prefigurative politics' refers to the general shift in emphasis away from attempts to seize the state apparatus or influence existing socio-political systems and towards the construction of alternative futures in line with the aspirations animating social justice struggles (Holloway 2002). The politics of prefiguration that is so central to many contemporary forms of radicalism can be traced to peace, queer, anti-racist, student, feminist and ecological struggles (the so-called 'new social movements') that emerged in the wake of World War

II (Bagguley 1992; Polletta 2002). These struggles focused not only on influencing dominant political, social and economic institutions but on the transformation of the production of everyday life itself (Epstein 1991; Gordon 2002; Katsiaficas 2006; Polletta 2002; Ross 2002).

Our research-based intervention into the field of radical imagination and radical politics sought to address a central problem identified by recent scholarship on radical social movements in North America and elsewhere which has demonstrated that established methods and theories are insufficient to address the rise of a politics of prefiguration (Day 2005; Katsiaficas 2006; Polletta 2002). Examples of these prefigurative 'experiments in living otherwise' abound, including housing squats and co-operatives (Bockmeyer 2003; Katsiaficas 2006; Wachsmuth and Pasternak 2008), alternative educational initiatives (Day, De Peuter and Coté 2007), direct action collectives (Graeber 2009), Indymedia and other alternative media institutions (Atton 2003; Kidd 2003; Pickard 2006), social centres (Lacey 2005), non-status (Lowry and Nyers 2003) and Indigenous solidarity groups (Davis 2010), and 'critical mass' sustainable transportation activism (Blickstein and Hanson 2001). These types of radical initiatives and more are appropriately described as being marked by a distinctively 'anarchistic' character that has swept urban centres in North America and beyond since the late 1990s (Albertani 2002; Day 2005; Graeber 2009).

In our project, we have argued that the radical imagination defines not something that radical social movements like these *have* but something they *do*. Without visions of how the world might be different, struggles stagnate and decline. The radical imagination catalyses a shared sense of purpose and power and emerges from and contributes to encounters and relationships between actors. As a result, the study of the radical imagination necessitates the crafting of new methodologies capable of participating in this process, not merely describing it from afar.

Amidst the crisis maelstrom: research and the university

We began this chapter by considering how the trope of crisis can be used in the service of elite agendas to narrow our imaginations of what is socio-politically possible and bring us within the orbit of power. We also explored the relationship between these crisis-narrowed horizons, social research and the university as a key institution in the reproduction of the social order. At a historical moment marked by unending war, austerity, deepening inequality, social decay and an ever augmented repressive state apparatus, researchers and other intellectuals willing to offer ideological and technocratic fixes in defence of the dominant order are now hailed as 'public' social scientists par excellence. The trope of crisis has served as a whip in the hands of elites to reshape the way research, critical inquiry and education are configured and practised. Attacked publicly by the resurgent right as nothing more than a collection of overprivileged ivory-tower idealists, while simultaneously facing the defunding of post-secondary education and independent research, many academics have responded by feverishly attempting to demonstrate just how useful – even commodifiable – their work could be to those with their hands on the levers of power.

While it would be unfair to paint all calls for and manifestations of a 'public' social science as co-opted and degraded, we must critically interrogate the imperative to make social science 'public'. In an age of neoliberal attack on public institutions and the public sphere, the fetishization of 'public' research is, more often than not, a means by which academic inquiry is domesticated and defanged in the name of pleasing a spectral mass of people 'out there' who represent 'mainstream' interests, concerns, values and ideals. With increasing frequency, the requirement to 'make work public' is demanded by funders and administrators keen to instrumentalize or commercialize research. Speaking to constituencies beyond the ivory tower is clearly important. But we would all do well to remember that academic disciplines of any stripe are only valuable so long as they offer critical insights into our world, particularly insights that offer something tangible in terms of addressing the most pressing problems of our time. As traditional sources of funding for research and post-secondary education wither in the neoliberal desert, more and more universities, faculties, departments and academics have felt compelled to court private, vested interests, particularly from the corporate sector. In so doing they have often paid for their continued existence with their autonomy, integrity and critical capacity.

Beyond the hollow 'public' idealism of the neoliberal university, we can sometimes glimpse the mirage of something else, the common university to come. We explore this idea in more detail in Chapter 8, where we dream of a 'prefigurative methodology'. For now we merely want to frame our research project within a set of methodological and political quandaries germane to an age where all of us are enfolded within multiple crises. It can be tempting to imagine that the university, or at least the craft of research, remains immune to these crises, or that the appropriate response to crisis is to stage a heroic defence of the university, or of research, as the last truly noble pursuit in an age of crass and pathological instrumentality. We believe no such approach is possible; nor do we believe it to be desirable. Rather, we are interested in how we might accept the fact that we are all in the thick of (and participants in) a maelstrom of power that leaves no one immune or innocent, and explore what tactics and strategies are possible in our volatile moment.

TWO

Convoking the radical imagination

If the strategies of invocation and avocation that we discussed in the last chapter are limited, what might another strategy be? In this chapter, we discuss the dimensions, successes and failures of our attempt to 'convoke' the radical imagination in Halifax, Nova Scotia, a city where we have been conducting fieldwork, in various ways, since 2007. The strategy of convocation attempts to take seriously the very particular challenges, responsibilities and opportunities that accrue to academic social movement researchers. We want to craft a method that brings radical milieus together and creates spaces of dialogue and possibility. Like the strategy of invocation, it seeks to leverage the privilege, perceived legitimacy and peculiar autonomy of the university to valorize and enrich social movements. Like the strategy of avocation, it strives for a deeper integration with those movements, and to put the resources of academe at their disposal. But, unlike the strategy of invocation, its primary objective is not the production of academic knowledge. And, unlike the strategy of avocation, it does not surrender academic autonomy to social movements completely. Rather, the strategy of convocation encourages us, always on a case-by-case basis and with careful consideration of local circumstance, to create something novel: new zones of dialogue and debate, new forums of imagination and creativity.

We devised this strategy because of our belief in the importance of the radical imagination and our insistence that it is not a thing to be measured in individuals but a process to be observed and instigated in and between collectivities. We also devised this strategy to meet the challenges of studying social movements not as coherent and cohesive groups or organizations, but as 'radical milieus': diffuse assemblages of individuals, organizations and tendencies. In this chapter we explain and reflect on our experiment with this strategy.

Context and practice:
the Radical Imagination Project in Halifax

When we began our research project the Halifax radical milieu was marked by a particularly rancorous split between more moderate and more militant activists in the city, one which fractured relations of cooperation and solidarity that had been built through the work of activists and organizers over many years. The catalyst for this split lay in a particular protest event that took place in Halifax in June 2007. During the summer of 2007, Halifax played host to the Atlantica summit of Canadian and US political and economic leaders eager to transform the Northeastern Seaboard into a free-trade zone. Complete with a race to the bottom for labour and environmental standards, the goal of the summit was to lay the groundwork to turn the region into a 'gateway' for goods produced in Asia to enter the continental United States while simultaneously accelerating energy exports to the USA (Sinclair and Jacobs 2007). This summit was an obvious target for radical activists in the Halifax area and beyond given the neoliberal paradigm it exemplified, but the protests themselves resulted in what almost all participants and observers report to be an unqualified disaster. Entrenched disagreements over protest tactics and inadequate collective participation in the protest planning process led to a ruinous polarization between more conventional protesters and a 'black bloc' committed to clashes with police. Veteran activists note that the event ruptured relations of trust and cooperation that had been building for decades, poisoning the local ecology of radical activism.

This defeat was compounded, in 2010, by the election of the New Democratic Party (NDP), the farthest left mainstream party, to Nova Scotia's legislature. While most of the members of the radical left in Halifax had long been distrustful of the tepid social-democratic politics of the NDP, many had actively or passively supported the party, whether out of a sense of personal obligation to various candidates or campaigners, or out of a sense that their participation and possible victory in the electoral realm might help shift politics and discourse leftwards. The NDP ran on a relatively conservative platform and, when elected, disappointed many of their left-wing supporters by failing to meaningfully challenge the neoliberal paradigm, exacting cuts on health care, education, social services and other elements of the welfare state. While veteran activists were not surprised (given that the precedent had been set in many other Canadian provinces where the NDP had been elected), the political failure of this supposed leftist electoral 'victory' opened up a moment of soul-searching. If electoral politics (at least in their current form) could not solve the crisis, what could?

In the wake of these fractures, fragmentation and sectarianism reigned in the Halifax activist community; however, it offered a unique opportunity to study the radical imagination in action as radical movements sought to reconstitute themselves in a relatively small socio-political space. In the midst of this historical low point for social movement activity, strategies focusing on simply observing, commenting on, or even going to work within the fabric of social change struggles no longer appeared, to us, as viable or effective routes for engaged research. Instead, through the Radical Imagination Project, we have sought to mobilize the (unjustly) privileged, relatively autonomous space of academic research in order to facilitate what activists and movements rarely create for themselves: an intentional and non-sectarian space and process capable of summoning into being the radical imagination (see Haiven and Khasnabish 2010).

The Radical Imagination Project goes further than most ethnographic accounts of social movement activism in the sense that it seeks not merely to observe but to convoke the radical imagination, to catalyse a public dialogue between activists and organizers based on the recognition that the radical imagination is a dialogic process. The project advanced in three phases.

Over the course of two years, we spoke with and catalysed conversations between emerging and elder activists, those who were considered central movement participants and those on the margins. Our research collaborators (as we prefer to think of our 'interviewees') worked in a variety of organizations on a range of issues and included employees of environmentalist NGOs, street punks, anti-racist and Indigenous organizers, book publishers, student activists, feminist militants, Marxist party members, radical academics, and anti-poverty advocates. Halifax is a city where most people in the radical milieu know one another, and where many activists participate in multiple organizations.

Our team's first active research phase began in September 2010 and was constituted by one-on-one interviews and focus groups, supplemented by our attendance at movement events and a self-reflexive process involving regular team debriefings and the keeping of research journals. We carried out project outreach by placing advertisements in local alternative media sources (print, radio and online), postering and pamphleting in public spaces, the use of pre-existing research and activist connections with groups and individuals, and word-of-mouth participant recruitment.

Our more than thirty one-on-one in-depth and open-ended interviews with diverse members of the Halifax activist community focused on asking our research collaborators to reflect on their own political biographies, notable moments of radicalization, perceptions of opportunities and barriers to radical social transformation, and visions of the future. Through these interviews we aimed to collect an archive of radical activism in Halifax at a particularly crucial time marked, on the one hand, by movement reconstitution and, on the other, by an ascendant right-wing agenda in society more broadly. We believe this kind of archive has utility not only for social movement scholars but for future generations of activists and organizers, particularly given the absence in so many grassroots, non-institutional movements of a place or process to intentionally curate the collective memory of struggle.

The interview phase of this project also constituted our initial attempt to provoke a wider dialogue among the activist community in Halifax. Flowing from the interview phase were two critical and interrelated processes. The first was the building of an ever-evolving online, interactive digital archive on our project website (radicalimagination.org). The online venture hosts publications emerging from the research, provides an online calendar of upcoming events related to the project, as well as an archive of audio recordings of our Radical Imagination Speaker Series (elaborated upon below). Still under construction due to the time-consuming work of transcribing and editing recorded interviews, the website will also host a dedicated space where we will curate thematically organized selected quotations from consenting interviewees as well as an hour-long audio documentary produced by one of our community research assistants that reflects on the project as a whole and features the voices and contributions of our research participants. We also aim to distribute the documentary more widely, particularly via activist and independent media. The website will also include spaces for discussion (anonymous and not) of the project's process and its outcomes as well as featuring invited contributions focusing on key themes and debates emerging from the project itself. In both the website's form and its content, we have sought to mirror the project's commitment to dialogue, creativity and engagement and to maintain it as an archive of social movement histories, which are too often lost as movements and their participants come and go.

The second phase of the project was the facilitating of a series of public events configured as 'Dialogues on the Radical Imagination', held in the winter and spring of 2011.

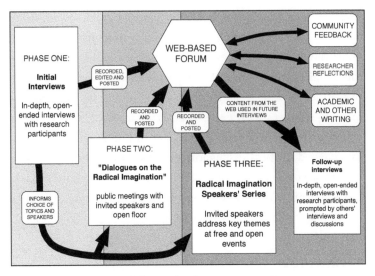

Diagram of the Radical Imagination Project

The Dialogues were free events, held in community spaces rather than academic ones, and were open to the public. Based on the most salient themes and cogent voices to emerge from the interview phase, certain research collaborators were asked to sit on a panel at each Dialogue. Rather than simply being a forum for the research team to present our analysis to the community, the Dialogues allowed panellists to offer short and often provocative statements based on personal experiences of organizing and activism; these served as springboards for moderated, open discussion among research team members, project participants and members of the broader community. Lasting two hours, each Dialogue focused on a key 'problematic' or theme that had emerged across the interviews: building resistance and alternatives in an age of austerity; the relationship between anti-capitalism and struggles against other structural oppressions; and the question of how we organize effectively for social change. These Dialogues served as a gateway into the project's final phase, which is ongoing, which involves inviting speakers with experience in a variety of radical struggles outside of Halifax to participate in public talks, followed by engaged, critical discussion sessions. Our intention was to bring a selection of perspectives and experiences not necessarily found within the local context in order to further stimulate the dialogic process of convocation.

Taking stock

We have sought to provide an overview of our attempt to build a research-based intervention capable of participating in social change processes and not just cataloguing them. As is often the case with social research, we are left with at least as many questions as answers. We are convinced that our attempt at developing this dialogic, engaged process has already been productive in terms of generating discussion and possibilities concerning the ways engaged research may be used as a radical social change tool, particularly at a time when the horizons of what is socio-politically possible are obscured by crisis, austerity and ever more repression of dissent. In the following chapters we take up some of the most important lessons and insights we have gleaned from the Radical Imagination Project. Here, we want to reflect on some of the issues relating to engaged research and the political that confronted us over the course of this project.

First, an admission: nothing in our research at the time gave us even a hint at the emergence of the Occupy movement beginning in September 2011. Occupy came to Halifax in October 2011 with a lively occupation of the Grand Parade grounds in the heart of the city's downtown core, involving many people totally new to the activist milieu. Our previous research did not detect the subterranean currents of dissent that would ultimately explode into Occupy, and this should give us pause and compel us to consider how our own positions even as engaged, reflexive and attentive researchers are bound up with their own assumptions, prejudices and unseen contradictions. Or perhaps we did not miss this percolating dissent; rather, it is possible that our own initiative simply was not built to intersect with this gestating movement. No matter how committed, grounded, self-reflexive and rigorous, engaged researchers cannot ever afford to assume that our interventions and initiatives are more than situated, partial perspectives on the broader terrain of socio-political struggle and possibility. This does not make them any less valuable, but it should remind us of the importance – analytically and politically – of humility.

Since the design stage of this project we grappled with the question of whether conducting research like this plays a role, however unintentional, in facilitating the surveillance, repression and demobilization of the very social justice activists with whom we work. By posting an online archive of activist interview material, for example, are we not providing a searchable intelligence database free of charge to the security apparatus? We are intensely aware of the utility of information that illuminates the fabric of radical social change movements to those who would seek to disrupt them. At the same time, informed both by our analytical perspective and by our political experience, we are equally convinced that if systems of violence, exploitation and repression are to be successfully challenged, it will only be through mass collective action capable of challenging the operation of power and building alternatives to it. That being so, we are convinced that the only way to convoke the radical imagination and cultivate the capacity for this kind of mass counter-power is to do so in a way that engages people in an accessible, collective and public way. From an analytical perspective, this approach also proves to be methodologically rigorous and robust, providing the framework for productive encounters to take place between people committed to a variety of social justice struggles, facilitated to varying degrees by the research team.

Any information collected relating to the work of activists, organizers and their groups is undoubtedly of interest to those invested in defending the status quo. Our project has quite intentionally not collected anything that might be considered 'operational information' as it relates to activists and their collective struggles. Indeed, the project's focus has always been about facilitating a collective process to catalyse a new radical imagination in Halifax, rather than collecting information about strategies, tactics and the balance of forces among movements. Of course, we have also sought to strictly protect the confidentiality of all our community partners and the anonymity of those who have requested it.

None of this eliminates the risks regarding how others might choose to use our research, but it does, we believe, mitigate against them. We also hold to the conviction that having these conversations and encounters is now more necessary than ever, but only if they truly do play some role in inspiring a new radical imagination and movements capable of acting on it. If not, they are either purely academic exercises or group therapy sessions, both of which may have their utility but which are also insufficient for meeting that goal.

Community responses

There were, of course, positive outcomes to the project reported back to the research team by our collaborators. Many found the initial interview phase engaging and stimulating, providing a rare opportunity to articulate and elaborate their political biographies and ideological orientations. Most appreciated this unconventional format of social movement dialogue and saw value in the idea of creating a collective archive accessible to the public and other activists, although in this regard some expressed scepticism that people would take the time to read each others' interviews or that the website would provide a meaningful forum for dialogue. On this point, others felt that notions like 'dialogue' and 'debate' were overvalued and could even perform the function of obscuring profound ideological and personal tensions within the activist milieu. Some members of that milieu refused to participate, or chose to participate anonymously, either for fear of state surveillance or out of concern about the response from what they perceived to be a highly judgemental community. Indeed, during the course of one-on-one interviews, several participants asked for the recorder to be turned off or that segments be deleted when they had spoken frankly about other individuals or specific organizing experiences. To some extent, this reflects the deep fractures still marking the activist milieu in Halifax and the limits of a process like ours to help members of this community to work through them.

From a methodological perspective, many participants criticized our sampling approach, suggesting that 'activism', 'radicalism' and social movement participation cannot be limited to those who self-identify as such, noting that such self-identification highlights the voices of those with social privilege – in the context of Halifax, these voices most frequently belonging to university-educated white youth. Not infrequently we were also faced with scepticism about the goals of the project itself, with more than a few activists articulating the belief that the project was designed to accumulate academic capital first and foremost and only secondarily benefit the community. In the same vein, several participants challenged the ethical framework of the project, claiming that although it was committed to engaging primarily anti-hierarchical social movements and had been designed with considerable community consultation, it nevertheless lacked formal mechanisms ensuring community ownership and oversight.

The Dialogue sessions produced similarly ambivalent outcomes. On a positive note, many participants stated that they appreciated taking part in a collective process aimed at discussing 'big' ideas and sharing political experiences, motivations and commitments in a space they perceived to be neutral. Many agreed that such spaces were relatively rare in their political experience, and also reported being inspired by the sessions and having their imagination radicalized. From our perspective as engaged researchers, we were pleased with the relatively high attendance at each session (between thirty and forty in each case), as well as the fact that many participants returned for all three sessions. But the Dialogue sessions were also subject to some criticism. For instance, some more experienced activists and organizers expressed frustration that while the Dialogues generated some provocative and wide-ranging discussion, they did not leave social movements much farther ahead in terms of solidarity or generate any strategic insights for forward movement. It should be noted, however, that forging solidarity and answering tactical or even strategic questions was not actually the goal of the sessions. Quite the opposite, in fact: the Dialogues were intended to make differences and disagreements more stark and transparent and to stimulate broader collective visions of socio-political possibility. Other participants raised objections with respect to our choice of featured speakers, who, due to reasons ranging from schedule conflicts to lack of interest, were often less diverse than we had hoped for, in terms of both their backgrounds and their organizational and ideological positions.

For the more experienced activists and organizers, the open nature of the Dialogues restricted their ability to engage one another directly in more sophisticated – and often fractious – strategic debates for fear of alienating or confounding less seasoned attendees. Compounding this, many of our participants from marginalized constituencies – queer, African-Nova Scotian, and even women – felt that the events' open-ended and lightly moderated format did not allow for an effective exploration and practice of anti-oppression politics. This concern was highlighted during the second Dialogue session which aimed to stimulate a critical discussion about the intersection of oppression and capitalism and oppression within social movements.

While the free-flowing discussion was lively, it rested almost exclusively on the question of capitalist oppression and exploitation and conspicuously avoided the more vexing – and much less frequently engaged – issue of movement participants' own behaviours and practices as they relate to the reproduction of systemic oppressions both within and outside of movements (see Chapters 5 and 6). This issue came to the fore again in the lead-up to the final Dialogue session as issues of sexual aggression, patriarchy and sexism within the movement were brought up by a number of activists. Many participants felt that the project ought to commit time and resources to assisting the community in working through these dynamics. We have yet to succeed in crafting an effective, collaborative, and engaging way of doing so.

On the whole, however, we were pleased by the community response to the Radical Imagination Project. While not every activist, organizer or self-identified radical in Halifax has responded to the project with unequivocal enthusiasm, many were excited to take part in it; others saw a qualified utility in it; some met it with lack of interest and scepticism. Given that the objectives of the project were never instrumental or tactical, along with our conviction as researchers that the radical imagination is both a subterranean current in collective thought and an everyday manifestation and process, the impacts or outcomes of the project are difficult to quantify. Nevertheless, in the feedback we have received, many of those who took part report positive experiences and a broader capacity to envision the future. However, from our perspective as researchers, we also feel that the critical discussions carried on through the phases of this project did not achieve the kinds of innovation, provocation and inspiration we had hoped for at the outset. Indeed, from our perspective – further confirmed by the reflections provided by the participants with whom we spoke – the critical, engaged discussions our project aimed to catalyse were largely a rehashing of debates that have circulated in radical milieus since at least the 1960s. While this by no means invalidates the usefulness of the project, it does suggest that our research-based intervention aimed at convoking the radical imagination did not go far enough. Further time and critical reflection are necessary for us to explore how we might have crafted a process of collective, dialogic engagement differently in order to push past these well-trodden discursive paths. Indeed, as the project proceeded, it was the conviction of some members of the research team that, despite our committed attempts to create a novel, radicalizing process capable of convoking the imagination, we simply did not push far enough beyond a relatively conventional qualitative research paradigm and so never managed to facilitate a truly collective, dialogic space or process.

This realization, in part, is what stimulated the ongoing third phase of this project in which we are hosting lectures and workshops, with speakers from within and outside of the Halifax context whose perspectives, analysis and experience lend themselves to our focus on the radical imagination and radical social change. Working with community partners to identify potential speakers of interest, this third phase involves bringing speakers to Halifax when possible, and making use of online teleconferencing when not, in order to allow these speakers to share their perspectives with participants. The first iteration of the Radical Imagination Speaker Series ran in

January 2012 and featured Dr Glen Coulthard, a member of the Yellowknives Dene First Nation and an assistant professor of the First Nations Studies Program and the Department of Political Science at the University of British Columbia. In two talks on consecutive days – one aimed at a broader community audience, the other held at Dalhousie University and attended primarily by academics – Coulthard focused on Indigenous struggles, place-based imagination, decolonization, and the fabric of radical struggle for social change in the context of the Canadian state. The talks were recorded and the audio was posted to the website of the Halifax Media Cooperative, a popular grassroots venue for citizen journalism and critique.

The second instalment of the speaker series took place in August 2012 and featured Dr Gary Kinsman, a long-time queer liberation, anti-poverty and anti-capitalist activist and a professor of sociology at Laurentian University in Sudbury, Ontario, Canada. Kinsman's talk, held in a public library in the historically marginalized but currently gentrifying North End of Halifax, was entitled 'Queer Liberation History: Resisting Capitalism and Oppression and Challenging the Neoliberal Queer'. Much like Coulthard's talks, Kinsman's presentation generated considerable interest in the activist community and was also digitally recorded for archival purposes.

In November of 2012, Max Haiven, one of the co-authors of this book and a co-director of the Radical Imagination Project, gave a presentation based on his experiences working with Occupy Sandy, the grassroots mutual aid response to 'superstorm' Sandy that ravaged the New York metropolitan area in October of that year. Focusing on the way the idea and practices of the commons provided an antidote and a means of resistance to 'disaster capitalism', Haiven's presentation generated fruitful dialogue on the questions of community capacity-building and the role of the state in the age of austerity.

In the fall of 2013, the series continued. Silvia Federici and George Caffentzis visited in October, delivering a series of lectures on the politics of the commons, taking up themes including women and the global economy, the politics of work under capitalism, anti-debt struggles, and the concepts of commoning and enclosure. Their visit was held in conjunction with a festival to celebrate the 250th anniversary of the Halifax Commons (a large parcel of land in the middle of the city, some of which remains parkland and some of which has been privatized or used for hospitals and other public buildings) and with the Halifax People's History Conference, organized by a non-sectarian, grassroots, anti-capitalist initiative called Solidarity Halifax. This latter group emerged as our primary research phase was drawing to a close, and represents (as of writing) an exciting and quite successful initiative.

In November 2013, the Radical Imagination Project hosted lectures by Harsha Walia, a Vancouver-based feminist and anti-racist organizer and author of *Undoing Border Imperialism* (2013) noted for her work with No One Is Illegal, a direct-action collective committed to migrant justice. Walia's first public talk focused on feminism, anti-oppressive practice and solidarity, while the second was about people's movements challenging border imperialism. Both generated significant interest within the local social justice community. The following week, we co-hosted the launch of the book *Yellow Ribbons: The Militarization of National Identity in Canada* (2013), by local author A.L. McCready.

We are currently planning for several more instalments of the Radical Imagination Speaker Series. Our hope for this stage of the project is that voices from outside the Halifax community will catalyse and provoke new ideas and conversations which might not be possible or plausible within the community itself. This is not because our research participants lack the necessary imagination but because, as we discovered in our interviews, dialogue sessions and conversations, complicated personal and political histories render some important issues and debates essentially taboo. Outside perspectives and voices allow us to navigate fractures and fissures that otherwise might be impassable.

Convocation and the research horizon

We have offered an overview of our attempt to chart an alternative approach to committed, engaged social science practice. While it should be abundantly clear that the Radical Imagination Project is far from perfect, as an experiment in innovating an ethnographically based research method capable of not only documenting social movements and social change struggles but actually engaging them, it has proven promising. More than this, our project has also demonstrated that it is possible to conduct engaged, committed research that participates in efforts to realize a better world without sacrificing academic rigour or our imperfect autonomy as researchers. Given its commitment to exploring living social realities rather than conceptual abstractions, ethnography seems to have something important to offer to visions of how engaged research might contribute to broader communities outside of our fields of expertise and the university. The systemic forms of violence, inequality and exploitation shaping our world today cannot be addressed through technocratic fixes or through the proper application of expert knowledge. In fact, if the latest convulsions of global capitalism reveal anything it is that our systems of knowledge production and application have largely become far too enmeshed in the status quo and the dominant interests it reflects. What is needed, then, at least in part, are approaches to critical research that seek not only to describe a given phenomenon or to ruminate endlessly on its complexity but to participate in facilitating collective, grassroots ways of envisioning and, ultimately, materializing alternatives to structures of violence. In contrast to the co-opted and toothless idealism of 'public' social science, we want to imagine the radical horizons of a common research. Critical and engaged research grounded in rigorous, principled methods matters – perhaps now more than ever given the ideological, mystifying nature of the ascendant right's assault on basic principles of reason, justice, democracy, equality, freedom and peace. And while it is not the only or even the most important piece in the social change puzzle, it has the potential to assist social justice struggles in ways that go beyond providing good information or reliable analysis. Today we face a concerted attempt to enclose our collective imagination of the politically possible by those with vested interests in diminishing our capacity to envision and live otherwise. In the face of this, critical social research must not only help reveal structures and systems of violence, exploitation and domination – as well as those who benefit from their perpetuation and those who are consumed by them – it must also contribute to people's capacity to imagine and forge paths beyond them.

In other words, and in ways that we shall take up in more detail in the following pages, we want to envision a solidarity research strategy that opens up new commons for the imagination. In a moment when knowledge is everywhere enclosed, instrumentalized, colonized and commodified, we are curious about how research can be about more than crafting finished products and can participate in cultivating community and transforming the imagination more broadly. The strategy of 'convocation' we have outlined is merely one experiment, and one (imperfectly) crafted for the particularities of the situation in Halifax, but it is based on a set of assumptions or ideals we believe should be at the core of solidarity research more generally. Key among these is the realization that social movements are always already researching; they are always already producing knowledge and reflecting (see Conway 2004). Rather than imagining that the researcher must bring the reflexive impulse in from the outside, we see the merit in beginning with the idea that the researcher can help catalyse, refine and render more rigorous and productive the forms of movement research already in action. As we shall explore in the coming pages, grassroots reflexivity, analysis and 'research' often break down, which can often lead to poisonous or at least unproductive movement dynamics, especially in radical milieus where cohesive, coherent and well-organized movements do not exist.

A second key ideal here is the faith that (as we shall explore more fully in the next chapter) much can be learned from failure, or, more accurately, from the gap between success and failure within which most movements dwell. It is for this reason that we elected to conduct our fieldwork in Halifax, a city by no means notable for the vibrancy or power of its radical movements. While it is always tempting to fixate on those areas of the world where struggles for peace, justice, equality and autonomy are 'winning', we think a more honest and potentially more useful analysis can come from working with the much more common activist experience that, at least on the surface, appears to be marginalization, stagnation and disappointment. Our strategy of convocation is aimed at working with movements in this state, rather than in their more triumphant moments.

Finally, the strategy of convocation is one that sees the horizon of research meld with the horizon of radical activism. It imagines research not as a rarefied and detached process of knowledge production – or, worse, knowledge extraction – but as an intimate part of social relations. As we discuss in the following chapters, convocation is driven not by some idealism about what research can be in the present. Indeed, it accepts and embraces the fact that research is never perfect, never complete, and never unproblematic. Rather, it builds a research agenda based on a certain strategic optimism about the future. In the society to come, the society both social movements and their solidarity researchers want to create (though one that no one person can articulate or imagine in its entirety), what would the role of research be?

PART TWO

Dwelling in the hiatus

THREE

The crisis of reproduction

During the Radical Imagination Project, we asked our research participants a particularly provocative and open-ended question: 'what would it mean to win?' In asking this question – borrowed from the title of a collected volume edited by Turbulence (2010), a radical collective of scholar-activists – we hoped it would help illuminate what allowed or motivated radical activists to continue their work even when and where it felt hopeless. We wanted to think through the ever-receding horizon on which they fixed their gaze and towards which they walked. We wanted our participants to move outside their everyday work and tactical activities and tell us what drew them to the future, to tell us about the hoped-for destinations that inspired their struggles. We anticipated a variety of inspiring answers. We were perhaps too optimistic. Almost invariably, this question was met with a pregnant pause, a break or a hiatus in the interview. It was not a comfortable silence. There was, to our minds, an interval of shame or embarrassment. Was it because our collaborators' heads were filled with images of impossible private utopias, so much at odds with their self-presentation as grizzled, pragmatic veterans of social movement struggle that they hesitated to articulate them? Or, more terrifyingly, was it because in the place where we expected to find fully articulated robust visions of victory, we found something far more sparse, emaciated and weary?

After the pause, most of our collaborators responded in one of two ways. Some began to articulate more or less complete and coherent visions of their desired futures. Some expressed comprehensive ideas of a new society, though largely in terms of broad values or ideals rather than practices or institutions. For instance, some talked about 'winning' as creating a world without poverty, or without sexual violence, or where education and housing were social rights, not commodities. In general, these visions were articulated piecemeal, and mostly in the negative: the future would be free of the various plagues of the present. The other form of response was a certain wryness or pragmatism. These participants imagined success as small victories in the here and now: the defeat of a certain law or policy, a successful campaign to forestall an eviction, or the radicalization of one more person.

Rather than focusing on these responses, we are interested in the possibility that lies within the uncomfortable pause, the moment of hesitation before the articulation of a vision or the rejection of the question entirely. Imprisoned Italian communist leader Antonio Gramsci is famously said to have characterized the plight of the radical as 'pessimism of the intellect, optimism of the will'; we're interested in the comma that separates the two phrases. As social movement researchers, we all too often think we need to analyse the successes and failures of movements. Indeed, those of us committed to social movements as more than just sources of data often believe it is our responsibility to provide this information to movements: what works? what doesn't? why? what lessons can be learned? which tactics and strategies for making radical change are effective and which are not? By contrast, in this chapter, we address the pregnant pause, the hiatus, as a fruitful and important moment. Rather than seeing it merely as an absence, we want to explore the hiatus to understand what dwells there. What if, rather than rushing to measure movements and research by the yardstick of dominant notions of success and failure, we take advantage of the hiatus to find another way out? Our wager is that there is a great deal that scholars and social movements can learn if, rather than seeking to analyse movement successes or failures, we instead attended to the uncomfortable pause between success and failure. What becomes possible within the hiatus and what can solidarity research contribute to it?

Within psychoanalytic practice, pauses or breaks in testimony are said to reveal fundamental contradictions in the ego. We largely reject any psychologizing or psychoanalytic approach – all too often these individualize what are in fact social and sociological problems. But we do think there's value in analysing and questioning this fraught moment. We believe that the 'hiatus' represents a collective moment caught between success and failure, and one where we can reimagine what success and failure mean. All too often, we argue, social movements (and those who study them) inherit and reproduce conventional and unquestioned notions of victory and defeat, notions that, in our observations, set up a pattern of unrealized expectations and pessimism. In this section, we want to suggest that social movements and solidarity researchers can reimagine success and failure in much more complex and productive ways. The 'hiatus' we encountered in our research is not the anomaly, it is the norm, but this might not be as regrettable a state of affairs as we might be tempted to assume.

We interpret the hiatus as symptomatic of two overlapping crises of 'reproduction'. The first is a crisis in the reproduction of human beings and their social lives, what Marxist feminist scholars have critically explored as an ongoing, never-ending 'crisis of social reproduction' under capitalism (Federici 2012). This crisis is defined by the way that we are all caught up in a system of capitalist, patriarchal, homophobic, white supremacist exploitation that is itself always fundamentally in crisis. Not only does this system evidence a perpetual economic, ecological, social and political crisis; it places all our lives in crisis as we struggle, each in our own way, to find equality, freedom, peace, security, happiness, love and meaning in a world torn apart by hierarchies, greed, abuse, corruption and the grinding unfairness of it all. Beyond merely a biological connotation, the idea of 'reproduction' here speaks to the way social relationships, social ideas and social bodies are always being reproduced, and it forces us to attend to the often overlooked *work* we and others do to reproduce our social relations. Reproduction doesn't simply mean repetition, but it does reframe our conception of struggle and resistance to encompass attempts to reproduce social life otherwise, to change the patterns and cycles of both individual and collective life towards the reproduction of values like solidarity, compassion, equality and empowerment, and it foregrounds the necessary affective labour required to do so.

The second 'crisis of reproduction' we are thinking about is a smaller crisis of activists and social movements: the ongoing crisis that pervades the lives and collaborations of activists around the world, and certainly in Halifax and other cities in the global North. It includes the everyday crises we all face: not enough money, not enough security, difficult relationships, lack of access to the things we need, crises that have deepened and widened as neoliberalism and austerity whittle down the problematic gains of the post-war period (i.e. a welfare state, civil liberties and a modicum of regulation on capital). But it also involves a whole other range of problems that lead to activists and activist groups being unable to reproduce themselves or to do so well, with all the attendant crisis-laden consequences for larger struggles for social justice and social change. The crisis of activist reproduction is characterized by endemic egoism and loneliness, breakdowns in communication, burnout resulting from endless struggles against movement and individual entropy, and the costs and consequences of grappling with success and failure. We want to identify radical movements in the global North as caught between two crises of reproduction: the one that impacts and affects everyone in society (though in differential and unequal ways), and the crisis of movement reproduction which is tied to, but not exactly the same as, the broader social paradigm. By mobilizing the idea of 'reproduction' as an interpretive frame, we hope to show that social movements and social movement scholars can and should revisit their ideas of what constitutes 'success' and 'failure' for movements. Not only does this framing allow for an enriched understanding of social change and the significance of social movement activity, it also allows us to explicitly and critically consider what research with social movements can contribute to struggles for social justice.

As we discussed in Part 1, stories are a critical dimension of social movement practice. Storytelling keeps alive the legacies of radical struggles that have come before us, provides a vital vehicle for the circulation of social change strategies and tactics, and participates in cultivating the ground necessary for the forging of solidarities. Asking research participants to narrate their ideas and experiences has long been an important tool in the ethnographic kit, and recent research affirms that such narrations are not merely the verbalizing of an otherwise silent truth, but a creative, dialogic and performative experience (see Selbin 2010; Sitrin 2012; Wood 2012). In telling stories we don't simply explain the world as it is; we help bring the world into being. It was for this reason that we asked the fateful and fraught question, 'what would it mean to win?' We wanted to spur or stimulate the narrative imagination, to see our participants articulate how their pragmatic activist tactics in the here and now were part of larger strategies of resistance, and how these strategies worked in the service of and were inspired by broader visions of what social change could look like. We had hoped that this question would reveal what animated our participants politically and reveal the secret source of that mysterious river 'the optimism of the will'. In this, our question failed, but, as we shall explore in a moment, this failure was also a success.

What happens when narrative doesn't flourish, when it stutters or hangs? There is a key contradiction here. On the one hand, our research convinces us that narrative and story are crucial components of social struggles both for individuals and for collectivities. Yet so too, we argue, is the failure of narrative, the inability or reticence to tell the story. What narrative reveals is not a complete, coherent activist subject who plots her or his past, present and future with conscious and pragmatic intention, but a fractured and fragmented figure, one who is caught between individual and collective identity, between present and future, between destruction and creation, and between hope and despair. The crisis of narrative is, in this way, a mirror for the crisis of social and activist reproduction.

Crisis theory and social reproduction

The notion of the crisis of social reproduction has its roots in the Marxist interpretation of capitalist crises. Marx (1992) sought to show that the periodic recessions, economic collapses, stock-market tumbles (and their corollary increases in unemployment, poverty, homelessness and suicide) were not simply momentary systemic lapses but the norm within capitalism. Marx explained how elemental contradictions within capitalism ultimately led to systemic crises, crises that could not be avoided but only displaced or deferred. For instance, an elemental contradiction is that, unlike other, more diffuse systems of exploitation where labourers are segmented and working far apart (such as peasant- or slave-based societies), capitalism by its very nature concentrates a critical mass of oppressed and exploited people in order to facilitate their exploitation (Marx and Engels 2004). For this reason, Marx was optimistic that an emerging class of industrial workers concentrated in factories would make common cause and rise up against the system that exploited and oppressed them. To alleviate or defer this crisis the ruling class could (a) increase wages and improve working conditions; (b) use brutal force to crush worker organizing and resistance; or (c) invest in machinery so as to rely less on workers. Each 'solution' to this elemental contradiction, however, presented its own set of contradictions and crises (see Harvey 2006). Increased wages and working conditions reduced the amount of 'surplus value' capitalists could appropriate from the production process, leading individual capitalists to fall victim to competition and the system as a whole to stall for lack of capital to reinvest. Brutal repression is and has always been a key part of capitalist relations, but it often backfires, leading to increased militancy and resistance on the part of the oppressed and exploited. It also often relies on capitalists cutting deals with the state, which is itself susceptible to workers' influence – albeit in a minimal and moderated fashion, and then only in (putative) democracies. And while capitalists can and do try to replace workers with ever more sophisticated machines, and use technology to monitor and police workers, this, according to Marx, has very clear limits (see Perelman 1987). Only the 'living labour' of workers can be exploited. Workers can have their energy, creativity and dynamism harvested at ever greater rates; they can have their working conditions and rates of remuneration eroded; they can be chained in all kinds of pernicious and insidious ways to their capitalist exploiters – for example, through modern forms of debt bondage or dependency on the threadbare benefits tied to their employment status. For Marx, their labour is the source of wealth, the source of surplus value, and the corresponding debasement of their conditions of life multiplies the fruits of capitalist exploitation, but also renders the system susceptible to crises.

In contrast, the 'dead labour' of machines cannot be exploited (see Read 2003). Lacking any creativity and dynamic capacity, and requiring constant maintenance and innovation in order to offer advantages against competitors, the reliance of capitalists on machines displaces the crisis of worker agitation only to imperil the system itself. A reliance on technology and automation also leads to a crisis of 'overproduction', where the capitalist system as a whole produces too many of the wrong commodities, driving prices down and putting capitalists out of business. The apparent resolution of crises within capitalism is merely the elevation or displacement of crisis to another aspect of the system. Instead of paying higher wages or improving workers' conditions, capitalists might concede to the establishment of a welfare state, where through taxes workers themselves pay to ameliorate the worst conditions of capitalism (e.g. health care, education, pensions, social security, etc.). Rather than brutally repress workers directly at the site of production, capital might opt for a fascist government to carry out this task, or it might seek to sow seeds of competition and hierarchy between workers by fostering racism and xenophobia and/or by taking advantage of social divisions to transfer production onto more exploitable, marginalized and vulnerable workers (see James 2012). Yet another well-travelled route to overcoming or displacing crises of the falling rate of profit and overproduction is for capitalism to turn to colonialism, using racist violence to open new markets and new populations of exploitable labour.

The nuances of Marxist crisis theory are too complicated and contested to discuss here. The general idea, however, is that capitalism's elemental structure is such that its basic contradictions lead to endemic crisis. While such crises may appear as periodic economic downturns or recessions, these are merely the outward manifestation of a constant roiling turmoil in the very logic of the system. Rosa Luxemburg (2003), in her attempt to analyse the European situation in the 1920s, did the invaluable work of identifying how capitalist forces seek to displace crises in order to protect and accelerate the 'reproduction' of capital itself. So, for instance, she examines war as the logical outcome of the crisis of overproduction as European nation-states, seen less as autonomous political entities and more as containers and vehicles of competitive capitalist interests, hurl social resources at pure destruction in order to keep the capitalist system from collapsing. Wars not only conscript workers into jingoistic nationalism, subordinating them to the interests of the ruling class and nurturing an identification with those most directly responsible for their immiseration, they also allow for society's excess productive capacity to be 'wasted' on weapons and reconstruction. Were it not wasted, that elemental wealth might be demanded by workers, which would allow them to be self-sufficient and hence starve capital of its lifeblood (living labour). Capitalism can afford everything save abundance. A thought experiment is useful in illuminating this: what if all the world's military funding were to go to feeding the hungry, curing the sick and educating the young? What if all the 'innovation' of weapons and prisons were directed towards better ways of providing the necessities of life? What if peace enabled societies to build long-term prosperity, rather than focus on short-term, competitive economic growth? We begin to see the utility of war and violence in the 'reproduction' of capitalism.

Luxemburg similarly sought to show how the global expansion of European imperialism was key to capital's reproduction. Not only was capitalism driven by war and conquest, with all the advantages listed above; it also allowed capitalists to displace the worst kinds of work onto colonized populations, who effectively lived under fascist colonial rule, while reserving some of the benefits, such as cheap imported goods, for the workers of imperialist countries (Césaire 1972). Further, colonies opened up new markets for overproduced capitalist goods, providing useful dumping grounds for this excess production and further entrenching colonial dependencies. For instance, in India under British rule a robust indigenous textile industry was systematically destroyed and peasants barred from manufacturing their own textiles, so that Indians could instead be forced to feed raw cotton and other materials into the British manufacturing system only to buy back the finished products at a monumental mark-up. Gandhi's famous Khādī movement centred on the boycotting of imported British textiles and the building of Indian self-reliance through the rekindling of hand-spun hemp production as a means to confront and overcome colonialism.

For Luxemburg the reproduction of capital was a key means through which one can understand all those aspects of the capitalist economy not directly related to the struggle between capitalists and workers. It is in this vein that the term 'reproduction' was taken up by Marxist feminists beginning in the 1960s. Maria Mies's (1986) book *Patriarchy and Accumulation on a World Scale* stands as emblematic of this approach. In it, Mies argues that Marx and subsequent Marxist scholars have been so fixated on the relations of 'production' and the contest between (male, privileged) industrial workers and capital that they have missed the elemental labour on which production rests: the reproductive labour traditionally assigned to and performed by women. She asks the key question: who produces the most valuable commodity in capitalism, labour power itself? The answer is women. Not only do women biologically reproduce labour power by bearing children; under patriarchal relations, they also socially reproduce labour power by providing the family with 'free' reproductive services including cooking, cleaning, childcare, elder-care and sexual companionship. Indeed, the male 'producer' depends on, and in fact exploits, the female 'reproductive' labourer in the home in ways not unlike the capitalist exploitation of the worker in the factory. Mies argues that, throughout post-hunter–gatherer human history, reproductive labour has been gendered and exploited, acting as the devalued and invisibilized bedrock on which a superstructure of valued and esteemed 'productive' labour has been built. Under capitalism, the reproductive labour of subjugated women acts as a vital and key supplement to the male wage, and is in fact the real source of surplus value as all the work of care that goes into ensuring that workers are able to work is systematically erased. If workers cannot work because their physical and emotional needs are not met, who will produce wealth? If new generations of workers are not born, who will labour? Were the work of social reproduction to be acknowledged as vital and remunerated as labour, capitalism would be denied its accumulation of surplus value and be drained of its lifeblood. Marx (1992) argues that capital tends to remunerate workers only enough that they might reproduce their labour power, return to work the next day, and breed a new generation of workers. Mies (1986) points out that this relies upon the unpaid reproductive work of women, and that male industrial workers are effectively 'subsidized' by this free labour. In order to keep this labour cheap and plentiful, patriarchal social and cultural norms, entrenched by gendered and sexual violence, and an elaborate legal system built atop them, ensure that women are not permitted an economic and social existence outside of the domestic sphere. By the nineteenth century, the 'housewife' had become an icon of the reproductive labourer, whose entire social, personal and economic role was centred around the household, with the husband or father as the foreman.

Mies's writing was a part of a feminist movement that fundamentally transformed social relations for a vast number of women and men over the last third of the twentieth century. It drew on the same roots as the international Wages for Housework campaign, which, beginning in the 1970s, brought together women from across the world in a campaign that made an impossible demand: remunerate the reproductive work performed by women (see James 2012: 218–24; Federici 2012: 15–22). This campaign was launched in the last days of Keynesian capitalism when the state still functioned as a key mediator between capital and labour, ameliorating some of the worst consequences produced by the former and offering incentives for compliance for the latter. The demand made by the Wages for Housework campaign sought not only to highlight the unpaid and devalued reproductive work of women but struck at the deepest element of capitalism's contradiction: its reliance on this sublimated and subjugated stream of gendered energies (Weeks 2011: 113–50). Were capitalism actually to remunerate reproductive housework, the system would collapse: it would effectively demand that the surplus value generated by capitalism, which is the stuff by which the system reproduces itself, be redistributed, effectively collapsing the circuit of capitalist reproduction.

In the Wages for Housework campaign, we catch a glimpse of a movement with a more cunning approach to success and failure. Those who constituted Wages for Housework developed a strategy (indeed, a name) around a demand whose apparent impossibility not only revealed the exploitative nature of the system itself but forced the imagination beyond the tepid liberal terrain of rights and superficial and grudging wealth redistribution (Weeks 2011: 175–86). Of course, Wages for Housework 'failed' to win its stated objective, but in announcing its name and engaging in the struggle its members succeeded in fundamentally transforming the imagination surrounding reproductive labour, reframing the stakes and the struggle over social reproduction as essential to any committed anti-capitalism for generations of radical activists to come.

Wages for Housework was a radical stream of a highly diverse global feminist movement whose more liberal and institutionalized elements, as the 1970s advanced, became more and more integrated into the global capitalist apparatus. By the 1990s, corporate media, political elites and a raft of self-avowed intellectuals were eager to declare that feminism had run its course, having 'corrected' a key 'inefficiency' within capitalism by helping society overcome outdated prejudices and creating a space for women to compete in the free market (see Fraser 2013). The fact that women continued – and continue to this day – to do the vast majority of reproductive labour was grossly downplayed, as was the fact that, increasingly, much of this labour has entered into the formal capitalist economy in the form of the low-wage, highly precarious 'service sector' where elder-care, food preparation, child-rearing, sex work and even childbearing itself have become highly commodified (see Federici 2012: 91–113).

Silvia Federici, one of the founders of Wages for Housework, has been a key figure in updating and recalibrating Marxist feminist theories of social reproduction for neoliberal times, including a focus on new cycles and circuits of struggle. Some critics have suggested that Marxist feminist reproduction theory represented a second-wave feminist analysis and, by extension, that it suffered from the same limitations: a tendency to essentialize and homogenize 'women', reducing women's diversity to a set of imagined characteristics that excluded queer and trans politics and downplayed the persistence of other axes of oppression such as racism and classism as they intersected with the category of woman. Yet neither the history of Wages for Housework, nor its theoretical and analytical legacy, evidenced by authors like Federici and Mies, support such charges. From the perspective of this important intervention, women are identified as reproductive labourers not because of their 'essential' biological characteristics but because the capitalist, patriarchal binary gender system has assigned them this role historically and in the present. Indeed, reproduction theory alerts us to the economic 'necessity' under capitalism of the binary gender system, which is enforced through homophobia and transphobia, forms of political terrorism aimed at policing and reproducing the gendered division of labour. Reproduction theory represents the negation of this assigned role (just as communism promised the negation of the worker) and also broadens our scope of understanding to recognize that we are – regardless of gender and social location – doing some work of 'reproducing' social relations. Those who oppress and exploit are also doing their part to reproduce a system of oppression and exploitation. Even 'production' itself is a form of 'reproduction': workers in the factory, both in their interactions and in the things they make, are reproducing the fabric of social reality as they have come to know it (see De Angelis 2007: 65–78).

Socializing the crisis

It is from this perspective that we can identify our current moment as not merely one of economic and ecological crisis, but also of a crisis of social reproduction. This crisis has a variety of elements and it is borne differently depending upon a host of factors, including race, gender, sex, sexuality, age, ability, class and citizenship status. Globe-spanning in scope, this crisis lives its everyday life on the level of individual and collective social reproduction, and it is at this level that it is most obviously experienced. Worsening economic and social conditions weigh heavily on individuals, who are told (often and with conviction) that they must diminish their expectations, embrace precariousness, normalize never-ending crisis, trust authority, sustain the corporate state, and never question the status quo, all the while facing an increasingly chaotic and hostile world alone. In an ever more commodified world, bare survival exacts considerable psychological, emotional and physical tolls even as it demands the sacrifice of commitments, dreams and principles as the price of admission. The professional-managerial class – post-secondary-educated professionals such as teachers, professors, journalists, engineers, social workers, lawyers, doctors, artists and entertainers – often referred to inaccurately as the 'middle class' (an aspirational and poorly defined concept) and long regarded as a bastion of liberalism as well as a key cog in the engine driving consumer capitalism in the most affluent parts of the world, has over the last twenty years been eviscerated, joining the industrial working class in an increasingly meagre and precarious existence (Ehrenreich and Ehrenreich 2013). As Barbara and John Ehrenreich note, this has given rise to 'the iconic figure of the Occupy Wall Street movement: the college graduate with tens of thousands of dollars in student loan debts and a job paying about $10 a hour, or no job at all' (2013). Anxiety and despair thrive in the face of entrenched and widening inequality, precarious or non-existent work, a nearly completely unravelled social safety net, and constant reminders from the mouthpieces of power that this new 'austerity' will last not years or decades but generations.

We can add to this an endemic political crisis where the state, its welfare functions eviscerated through years of neoliberal cuts, increasingly turns towards policing, surveillance and repression, enacting what we lately have come to call 'austerity' on all spheres of life (Blyth 2013). More than four decades into a global political revolution which has seen government powers to discipline the market vastly eroded, the state today is wracked by a crisis of reproduction. Not only can it no longer 'afford' to reproduce its basic elements (infrastructure, social welfare, bureaucracy), but it responds to this crisis by attacking vulnerable populations. As Wendy Brown (2010) illustrates, the state increasingly looks to policing, surveillance of and enclosing populations to demonstrate its necessity, legitimacy and power to increasingly cynical populations. Seen from another angle, no longer the agent of corporatism and class compromise, the state today has become a core apparatus in a new era of accumulation by dispossession, its capacity for repression grotesquely augmented while its social development functions have been jettisoned (see McNally 2011). Within or against this hollowed-out state apparatus, neo-fascist, fundamentalist and ethno-nationalist tendencies flourish, promising meaning, security, order and an end to alienation through a return to a mythical moment *before* the crisis of reproduction, when we imagine that society actually worked (see Giroux 2004). The result is a culture of fear and loathing, where public issues like housing, health care, education, transportation and personal security come to be seen as private investments to which most individuals are woefully unable to contribute adequately.

This endemic sense of insecurity paves the way for the emergence of new forms of hatred, distrust and paranoia which feed on and fuel deep-seated prejudices and patterns of oppression. Racism, sexism, homophobia, transphobia, xenophobia, and a visceral hatred of the poor – indeed, of the Other – are cold comfort in a world without guarantees and further throw the lives of those targeted by these into crisis. We are in the midst of a mental health crisis of truly epic proportions, with a large and randomized study of adults in the USA conducted by the National Institute of Mental Health between 2001 and 2003 finding that 46 per cent met the American Psychiatric Association's criteria for having had at least one mental illness related to anxiety, mood, impulse control and substance abuse disorders at some time in their lives, figures well up from the previous decade (Angell 2011). In 2011, the US Centers for Disease Control and Prevention (CDC) reported that over the last two decades antidepressant use in the United States increased nearly 400 per cent (Levine 2013). In 2013, the CDC reported that the suicide rate among Americans aged between 35 and 64 had increased 28.4 per cent in the decade 1999 to 2010 (Levine 2013). While these figures are limited to the USA and do not account for new diagnostic methods, changing criteria for what counts as mental illness, and the impacts of drug company lobbying and marketing, they indict the dehumanizing effects of life under late capitalism in one of the most affluent – and unequal – societies on the planet.

To this we must add the spiralling ecological crisis, driven by the voracious appetite for raw materials and the combustion of hydrocarbons that characterize late capitalist consumer culture (Foster, Clark and York 2010). This crisis has led directly to a massive crisis of reproduction in many areas of the world, where droughts, floods, desertification, heat waves, massive and powerful storms, and increasingly volatile weather patterns have driven Indigenous people and other rooted rural communities from their lands and ways of life. Ironically and tragically, this transition has swelled the dispossessed and precarious population of urban centres – creating what Mike Davis (2006) has called a 'planet of slums' – whose ecological impacts intensify the crisis itself. While many of the most visible and extreme effects of the climate crisis have manifested in the global South, areas in the global North stand as harbingers of the dark road ahead. Chris Hedges and Joe Sacco (2012) call these large swathes of territory 'sacrifice zones' where the natural world and the life that inhabits it – including human life – are 'offered up for exploitation in the name of profit, progress, and technological advancement' (2012: xi). The Gulf of Mexico and large parts of the Canadian province of Alberta are two such zones, offered up to exploit deepwater oil reserves and bitumen respectively, with disastrous consequences for humans, other life and the planet. Another is the city of Detroit, Michigan, the largest municipal bankruptcy in US history, a testament to the bailout of corporations and the abandonment of people, and a city where those who can (mainly the white middle class) have fled while nature reclaims what used to be one of the paragons of capitalist industrial development. While the fabric of social life has frayed and climate catastrophe looms, our last bastions of collective defence against the fatal consequences of eco-social crisis, from health care to science in the public interest, from financial regulation to global climate accords, have been systematically defunded, shuttered and cast aside (Stuckler and Basu 2013). Chris Hedges (2013) describes this as a 'slow-motion coup d'état' orchestrated by political and economic elites and perpetrated against the rest of us, which has made a mockery of the protections supposedly guaranteed by the vestigial trappings of liberal democratic institutions remaining to us today.

What is key here is that under the present neoliberal/austerity consensus the endemic crisis of capitalist production is being downloaded onto the level of daily life and social reproduction. The consequences of the irreconcilable contradiction between the reproduction of capital and the reproduction of social life are nothing short of horrific. The reproduction of capital demands that the market expand into every corner of life, commercializing and commodifying most of the lifeworld. Since the end of the Cold War, capitalism has effectively saturated the planet, leaving almost no space outside its reach (Hardt and

Negri 2000). With no new spaces left to expand into, capital finds its outlet in the permanent, borderless war declared in the aftermath of 9/11. A war ostensibly directed against 'terror', it is, in fact, a globe-spanning biopolitical apparatus aimed at reshaping social life, disciplining, terrorizing or simply exterminating those in resistance and occupying the territories necessary to its reproduction (see Hardt and Negri 2004). Those of us not currently in the crosshairs of capital's war machine and not rendered entirely marginal to its reproduction are expected to commit, heart and soul, to increasingly precarious jobs where we work longer and harder, producing greater and greater wealth, for less. All this despite the fact that we live in an era of unprecedented automation, productivity and material abundance. Supporting the reproduction of capital is fundamentally at odds with the reproduction of social and personal life.

It is here that we must revisit our conception of 'success'. To be 'successful' in the present order is to somehow synchronize the reproduction of capital with the reproduction of our individual lives. Images of 'successful' individuals are constantly propounded in the news and entertainment media: the savvy university graduate who translates years of unpaid internships into a job in cognitive and creative capitalism; the glamorous career woman who somehow also cares for her children; the powerful businessman with his devoted wife and a social conscience; the model minority or 'good immigrant' who somehow both competes in the cut-and-thrust world of work and stays 'true' to his or her roots (in inoffensive ways); the upwardly mobile queer who succeeds in the boardroom, in the bedroom and at the mall; the enlightened NGO worker/

consumer who bicycles to work (with yoga mat strapped to his or her back), volunteers on weekends, and works on his or her novel at night; the crash-and-burn celebrity whose consumer narcissism is itself a (short-term) harmonization of market and the self. All these icons of 'success' are virtuosos of precarious times who have managed the impossible: not merely an enviable 'work–life balance', but a seamless integration of two levels of reproduction: that of the system and that of the individual. Failure, then, within this systemic framework is the universal condition of failing to integrate these two imperatives to reproduce. The workaholic, the burnout, the depressive, the part-timer, the underambitious, the overambitious, the greedy and the selfless – all are archetypes of a pathological culture founded on the contradiction of reproduction, one that is fundamentally driven by an impossible quest.

The death and afterlife of the middle class

The crisis of social reproduction, like the crisis of production, is a constant and indelible element of capitalist social relations and is likewise displaced (or, in today's corporate parlance, 'externalized') onto communities and individuals. During the Industrial Revolution, for instance, the crisis of social reproduction was displaced onto the working class, who were paid starvation wages, denied decent housing and clothing, and forced to work 80 hours or more per week. In the Keynesian period, the crisis was displaced onto women, who were increasingly expected to hold together households through unpaid domestic work, with tremendous personal and psychological consequences. The crisis was also displaced onto post-colonial nations, which, through political sabotage and compulsory debt, were subordinated to a neocolonial economic system driven by civil wars, dictatorships and IMF/World Bank-driven austerity regimes (Prashad 2007; 2013). Today, migrant labourers, sweatshop workers, Indigenous peoples displaced by mining companies or corporate cash-crop operations, and farmers enslaved to biotech and agribusiness corporations bear the heftiest weight of the global crisis of social reproduction. Yet, unlike in the Keynesian period, Western capitalist interests can no longer promise a slim minority of the world's population access to protection from the crisis through 'middle-class' membership in exchange for their docility and obedience. Or, more accurately, the slim minority of the world's population to be afforded middle-class belonging is no longer found in any one part of the world or in any one sector, and shifts with incredible volatility.

For two generations, the imaginary ideal of middle-class belonging meant a perceived freedom from the crisis of reproduction. Stable housing, health care, old-age security, the occasional escape from the drudgery of work through vacation, and access to education were supposed to afford middle-class families the ability to reproduce their lifestyle and privilege without fear or concern. Of course, the very notion of the 'middle class' is slippery and amorphous. In 2010 the US Department of Commerce abandoned any attempt to quantify it and instead began referring to it as an 'aspirational' identification so broad – 'home ownership, a car, college education for their children, health and retirement security and occasional family vacations' – that it excludes essentially no one (Ehrenreich and Ehrenreich 2013). This is especially so in a consumer economy driven by debt, where health, education, housing and consumer goods appear accessible, but at a terrible price. Nevertheless, its ideological properties render it a powerful myth to extract compliance from a key middle strata of workers who, while subject to the power of the owners of capital, are themselves invested with power to manage and discipline members of the working classes both in society and in the workplace (Ehrenreich and Ehrenreich 2013). Rather than a vague 'middle' class, Barbara and John Ehrenreich name this the 'professional-managerial class' (PMC), constituted by educated professionals (from teachers to social workers, engineers to doctors, IT workers to artists) coming to prominence during the early to mid-twentieth century and occupying a central role in capitalist accumulation since then. On the one hand, the PMC managed, regulated and otherwise controlled the conditions of life for the working classes in addition to designing the systems and technologies that directly shaped their conditions of labour. On the other hand, the PMC was also a liberal force in society, often countering the profit-maximizing desires of capitalists and sometimes expressing critical and even oppositional political perspectives relative to the status quo and seeking to advance a variety of social justice issues (Ehrenreich and Ehrenreich 2013).

The PMC remained a significant social force in the lead-up to and through the years of Keynesian welfarism, but once the neoliberal onslaught began in earnest in the 1970s the PMC and the middle class imaginary it embodied entered into crisis. As the capitalist class abandoned the class compromise that the welfare state had held together in a quest for revived rates of profitability, the PMC became a key target as government funding for a host of public services evaporated, jobs were moved offshore or simply eliminated, labour laws and unions were systematically undermined, and attacks on the industrial working class and the innovation of new, leaner production models reduced the need for an intermediate class of managers (Ehrenreich and Ehrenreich 2013). By the 1990s, the PMC had been decimated, with those members of the class remaining transforming themselves increasingly into apologists for and technocrats of power – a decisive transformation that Chris Hedges (2010) has decried as 'the death of the liberal class' and a fatal subversion of the liberal institutions once tasked with defending civil society.

Compounding this, volatile housing prices (where housing equity is seen as the single most important guarantor of middle-class reproduction), rising tuition fees, increased medical costs, the privatization of pensions, precarious or non-existent employment and social security, the rise of user fees for all manner of what were previously social entitlements, as well as the diminishing quality of state services, have all conspired to transform middle-class belonging into a site of anxiety and cynicism. At the same time, the myth of middle-class belonging has been marketed to more and more populations previously systematically denied access: lesbian and gay couples, independent women, racialized families, even whole segments of the population in 'developing' nations (now euphemistically renamed 'emerging economies'). Indeed, the ability to compete for middle-class belonging (and an imagined escape from the endemic crisis of reproduction) has been a key element of the neoliberal revolution, offered as a means to extract the consent, docility and complicity of the governed while repression is reserved for the rebellious elements who refuse to comply with the order. Most of those aspiring to middle-class belonging have sought not riches but a refuge from perpetual insecurity, but even as the myth has been marketed to a greater diversity of social subjects than ever before, its material bases have been thoroughly undermined. The result is a mirage of security and certainty that has left those aspiring to it wandering in a neoliberal desert, bereft of social solidarity and visions of alternatives and vulnerable to the hate- and fear-filled fantasies of the resurgent right.

In this sense, we want to identify the crisis of social reproduction and the hegemonic notions of 'success' as they circulate in the mainstream media and the neoliberal imaginary as inherently tied to the cultural and economic problem of the middle class. We do not wish to suggest, as do many liberal critics, that the problem with austerity and neoliberalism is that they undermine the possibility of the middle class. We do not believe the middle class should be expanded; we believe that all classes should be abolished. We believe that the rights, security, prosperity and sense of success that today are bundled up in how we imagine the middle class ought to be provided to everyone. Within post-war capitalism, the idea of personal and social 'success' has been tethered to the ideals of the middle class, and that belonging to the middle class has implied a certain immunity to the vicissitudes of the crisis of social reproduction under capitalism. As neoliberalism and austerity render middle-class belonging more and more elusive (even for those who possess professional jobs, significant assets, an education, etc.), failure to achieve or sustain middle-class belonging, or failure to enjoy what one anticipated would be the prosperity and security middle-class belonging afforded, has become a key political referent. This is the afterlife of the middle class: it lives on past its murder, haunting the minds of the living. In order for the radical imagination to thrive, it must loosen itself from the pathological fixation of the middle-class ideal.

The crisis of movement reproduction

Even though many of us disavow mainstream notions of 'success' and seek to reproduce our social lives otherwise, we remain the products (and, in many ways, reproducers) of the overarching contradiction of reproduction under capitalism. It is in this context that we want to reimagine and recontextualize both social movements and social movement study.

What emerges from all of these struggles within and against capitalist reproduction is the exaltation of a certain archetypical 'successful' activist, one seemingly immune to the endemic crisis of reproduction. To a certain extent, this archetype is part of the legacy of, rather than divorced from, Enlightenment modernism, a paradigm in which politics is cast as the domain of rational men debating in the public sphere. Given the way many social movements are forced to participate in the liberal political arena, the dominance of this archetype is not surprising. Often movements will select from among their ranks public spokespeople who appear to match this archetype most closely, further contributing to the power of the archetype as the paragon of successful activism. Often the person who can best embody the archetype is someone with a relative degree of privilege, whose life has been least constrained or wracked by the disjuncture between the reproduction of capital and the reproduction of social life, and who has had access to education, mental and physical health, and some degree of economic security.

Of course, this archetype is a fiction, or, perhaps more fittingly, a ghost, one that haunts movements and is symptomatic of the way the broader crisis of reproduction plays out in social movement contexts. A consumer capitalist system predicated on the endless expansion of capital into every sphere of life succeeds to the extent that it makes everyone feel inadequate, as if they are not successful but that the next act of accumulation just might get them there. This pathology is not eliminated by participation in social movements, no matter how radical their politics. Indeed, we need to examine how this pathology becomes internalized into movements (and into the radical fringes of academe as well) and reassess our concepts of success and failure to enhance and deepen solidarity.

Another dimension here is the incongruity between success as an activist and those broader meanings of personal success that orbit the phantom concept of the middle class. A common concern for many activists with whom we spoke was a fear of 'selling out' in order to make a living either in their chosen profession (and so be depoliticized by the need to 'professionalize' oneself to conform to industry expectations) or within the organized and institutionalized dimensions of activism and social movements (working for NGOs, universities, political parties or unions). Many activists, both on the outside and the inside of these occupations, worried that their need to earn a living and contribute to more mainstream organizations compromised their radical politics. The dissonance between successful reproduction of movements and of the self was acutely felt, especially by those of our interviewees who had or were anticipating having children or had communities of care that extended beyond themselves (for example, elders, disabled persons, or children in their lives who depended on them). Almost all interviewees acknowledged, in one way or another, that their own material and social security and their capacity for social reproduction were intimately connected to social justice and equality, and that the success of individuals in attaining the security of social reproduction under capitalism was essentially illusory. They expressed a great deal of shame and anxiety around the need or desire to achieve it for themselves alone.

It is here that we turn back to the reflection that we began with, the strange pause, the hiatus, after the question 'what would it mean to win?' Why was it that this moment of hesitation was almost always a preface to a list of absences ('a world free of racism', 'a world free of poverty') or a brusque retreat from the question itself and a turn towards the pragmatic day-to-day work of solidarity and resistance?

We turn to social movements not merely because they offer a means to transform our world but also because they offer a means of coping with a world of relentless and cascading humanitarian, ecological, social and political tragedy. Movements not only offer an ideological outlet, they offer a form of community and a source or support for identity in a world driven by impossible demands. This is true both of immersive movements that claim the whole subject (such as 'drop out' back-to-the-land communities, punk houses or lesbian separatist conclaves) and more casual and flexible movements. Because all these movements, to varying extents, challenge the mainstream capitalist version of 'success', they also offer their participants a reprieve from its imperatives, or at least support in enduring them. In other words, movements offer alternative spaces of social reproduction. They promise to be places where both individuals and communities can re-create themselves and find support for doing so at least partially outside the dictates of capital's reproduction. This is true even (perhaps especially) of rigid Marxist parties which insist their members sacrifice their 'bourgeois' comforts and pleasures and dedicate themselves body and soul to the struggle, but which scoff at more anarchistic attempts to 'be the change' and build a prefigurative politics. And it is also true of more organized and professionalized elements of movements which encourage participants to see their activism as a formal (sometimes employment) relationship, but which, in spite of such detachment, end up being hubs of common identity, feeling, friendship and reproduction.

Yet because movements are themselves products of the crisis of capitalist social reproduction, they can rarely self-consciously or self-reflexively admit to or contend with this important role they play in the lives of their participants. Most activists would rightly reject the idea that their movements are merely forms of therapy for wounded souls, and many groups actively discourage their members from taking solace in movement participation for fear it will lead to a culture of co-dependency and narcissistic catharsis. Most movements also understand, in different ways and to different extents, that the real source of our agonies is systemic, and that to solve these systemic problems requires a certain measure of self-sacrifice, meaning that activists should see their movements as effectively places of 'work' and salve their wounded souls elsewhere. It is not surprising in this context that the 'successful activist' archetype is so popular: it is the activist who, ironically, appears not to 'need' the movement, who does not rely on the movement for community and reproduction.

We are not suggesting here that movements merely become therapy groups (though we will, shortly, suggest we consider research a form of radical therapy). Far from it. But we do contend that movements are also places where the broader crisis of social reproduction plays out, and if movements are to *reproduce themselves* effectively and win the victories they desire, they must attend to this crisis. Part of this, we suggest, has to do with reimagining the meaning of success and failure.

FOUR

Reimagining success and failure

Judith Halberstam's *The Queer Art of Failure* (2011) offers us a useful place to begin reimagining the 'success' of social movements and social movement research. Halberstam asks us to consider: if 'success' is defined within an oppressive, exploitative and unequal society, can 'failure' be a liberatory practice? What are the 'arts' of failure that help undo the normative codes of success, especially in an age of rampant neoliberalism where personal advantage-seeking is held to be the key to prosperity, for both individuals and for society at large? For Halberstam, these themes are framed around questions of queer politics: if 'success' in gender performativity means being able to match one's performance of self to the given norms of gender and sexual behaviour, is the queer 'art' of bending, challenging or simply 'failing' to obey these norms not key to resisting the status quo? Halberstam is also interested in social movements, although through the lens of popular culture, noting the ways that many mainstream children's films (contrary to pessimistic readings that see them as purely hegemonic) actually narrate the failure of the sort of possessive individualism that is typically seen as 'successful' neoliberal behaviour. These films often depict the victories of those who we might consider 'failures', to the extent that these underdogs band together, make common cause, and challenge the overarching regime of success.

What might social movements and scholars of social movements learn from this approach? As we saw in Chapter 1, the academic field of social movement studies has, to a large extent, fixated on the question of movement success, even when that success has been understood less as quantifiable material and political gains and more as the fortitude and intensity of networks, or as transformations of subjectivity. Likewise, social movement scholarship that is considered 'successful' has typically produced observations and interpretations of movement achievements, or has managed to identify the causes of social movement failure. To embrace Halberstam's 'queer art' of failure would be to look to failures as potential sites of rupture and possibility.

Here another tool from critical theory can be equally useful. For Fredric Jameson (1976; 1981) and Donna Haraway (1992), the 'Greimas square' (named after the French semiotician) offers a profound heuristic tool for taking apart binary thinking and pluralizing the horizons of thought. While the rich and complicated semiotic theory behind the square is beyond the scope of this chapter, the basic idea is that tension between two (ostensibly) contrary concepts (in this case 'success' and 'failure') can be productively opened up by, in a sense, 'squaring' the equation and adding into the mix their 'contradictories' ('not-success' and 'not-failure'). The four terms can form a square, the sides of which offer up new possibilities for interpretation.

What is key is that 'success' is not the same as 'not-failure', and 'failure' is not the same as 'not-success'. The 'lines' in the square represent fruitful and provocative opportunities for

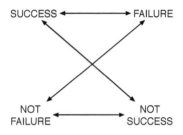

The Greimas square of success and failure

reconsideration. This is because, in Jameson's interpretation, the initial binary (success and failure) is 'ideological'. That is, it is an always partial, fractured way of understanding reality. The binary is forged within and tainted by the society of which it is a part. For instance, most critics will be familiar with the critique of the 'binary gender system': the binary of 'male' and 'female' exists as an element of a patriarchal gender system that allows certain traits, features and behaviours to be feminized (and devalued) and certain ones to be masculinized (and valorized) (see Butler 1990). The binary gender system grows out of a patriarchal society, and in turn shapes our thinking, performances of self and interpersonal actions in ways that see (most of) us reproduce a patriarchal society. To return to the Halberstams, our binary of 'success' and 'failure' is one defined by a normative social order, built by and reinforcing hetero-normativity, patriarchy, class exploitation, white supremacy and other modes of oppression. Within the limited 'success/ failure' binary, the absence of equal marriage rights for gays and lesbians is seen as a 'failure', and the gaining of these rights is seen as 'success'. But it is queer success within a heteronormative framework, which might lead us to question whether 'success' is all that 'successful'.

For Jameson (1976; 1981), in his Marxian approach to the Greimas square, the final reconciliation of the initial binary (some sort of possibility to transcend the ideas of 'success' and 'failure') is utopian: it exists just over the horizon of our thinking, possible only in an impossible world to come where we have conclusively overcome all the sorts of oppression and exploitation that frame (and benefit from) our current ways of thinking (see Haiven 2011b). Until then, it is the job of radical critique to deconstruct and open up supposed binaries and pluralize the sorts of options available for thinking and acting beyond the pregiven epistemic order. As such, each 'line' in the above square represents a key ideological tension. In the rest of this section we think through each in turn, first for social movements, then for solidarity researchers.

Social movements and the hiatus between (not-)success and (not-)failure

Key is that on each axis of the square a synthesis can emerge. For instance, on the original 'top' axis (2a), we might say that the synthesis of 'success' and 'failure' is that utopian moment when we no longer live by the sorts of binary expectations that are characteristic of systems of power ('rich' = success, 'poor' = failure), which we might call 'collective potential'. That is, it would be a world of freedom where individuals and groups were able to constitute and reconstitute themselves on their own terms. We suggest this is the sort of utopian moment of

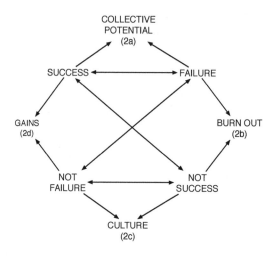

The expanded square of social movements

which social movements dream even though it is unlikely or impossible to realize. Yet we ought not to dismiss this receding horizon — it refocuses us on what the more substantive goal might be beyond particular ideas of success. As we have argued elsewhere (Haiven and Khasnabish 2010), the utopian dimension is crucial to social movement imaginations, even if movement actors can't fully or completely articulate what it might look like. In our square, we might be tempted to imagine that the left-hand synthesis (2d) is the most desirable, but the Jamesonian square (for by now it has gone well beyond Greimas's intentions) forces us to see that whatever emerges in this left-hand space (2d) is really only a limited possibility within (not yet beyond) the society that has created the initial opposition in the first place. That is, while 'gains' might be important, whatever fills that space will fall short of the more substantive and radical possibility at the 'top' of the square (2a; in this case, utopia).

So, on the left side of the square (2d), if we think of what social movement 'success' and 'not-failure' might mean, we might think of practical and material victories: success by a movement's own standards, or what we might call 'gains'. While not insignificant, what the square forces us to imagine is that a movement's own standards of 'success' may not, in and of themselves, be all that animate that movement. Hence the recognition that even when movements 'win', they rarely pack up and go home. For instance, the 2012 Quebec student movement succeeded in its stated objectives of turning back the planned increase in tuition fees, but the spirit of that movement lives on, both in campaigns for free tuition, groups that are confronting neoliberalism in other sectors of society, and in the affinity groups and friendships that formed during the strike and whose consequences are yet to be seen (Christoff 2013; Thorburn 2012).

Likewise, then, the square forces us to reimagine 'failure' as well. On the right-hand axis of our square (2b) we have the synthesis of 'failure' and 'not-success'. Not only are we thinking about a tactical or a strategic collapse and a failure of movements to reach their stated objectives and have their desired impact (the contrary to their concept of 'success'); there is also a more profound socio-psychological dimension, an absence of success. In the context of the movement actors we spoke to, we heard a lot about what our participants called 'burnout'. This meant not only pessimism about the possibilities for real change (success) but a weariness and cynicism that was wounding to the soul itself. Many participants reported being burnt out (and having withdrawn from activism), or having burnt out and recovered, or worrying about burning out in the future. Causes of burnout were numerous. Often it resulted from activists getting so caught up in the quest to succeed that they worked themselves too hard, typically coming to resent or becoming alienated from other movement participants who were not perceived to be pulling their weight. Others noted that for those with more advanced anti-oppression approaches, or who came from marginalized groups, the toll of dealing with ignorance and privilege from fellow activists was extremely taxing. Others confessed that the further they delved into movement participation, the less they had in common with non-activists, and that many relationships with non-movement friends and family members atrophied, leaving them isolated and alienated, especially in times of movement crisis and failure.

Based on these testimonies, our own experiences as activists and organizers, and a significant and growing body of activist reflection on self- and community care and burnout (Carlsson 2010; Loewe 2012; Padamsee 2011; Plyler 2006; Walia 2013), we think that activist 'burnout' is a key category that deserves much more exploration and consideration. Many elder and more experienced activists we spoke to revealed biographies that included periods of burnout, often followed by transitions into other movements or causes, sometimes radically different from those they had engaged in previously. Often this included a shift from 'activist' work (direct-action tactics, political lobbying and public education) towards 'organizing' and forms of self- and other-oriented care (including formal and informal social work, teaching, community mobilizing, or working for

NGOs). A few participants wryly and wistfully confided that, after burning out, they thought themselves done with radical politics for good, at least in any organized sense. In reality, we could not speak with many who had burnt out and left the milieu because they had completely severed ties with the activist networks that we were studying.

Burnout is key in part because it is so universal among radical activists. But it is also key because it is perhaps something radical social movement researchers do something about. Movements, we learned, often have difficulty offering the institutions, practices and spaces to help individuals avoid or return from burnout. Researchers interested in working with movements might be able to create or fortify these missing or crumbling elements of social movement culture. For instance, many of our research participants admitted that the semi-formal opportunity to talk through issues privately with researchers afforded them new perspectives and helped them work through metaphorical wounds, a sort of radical therapy. We also tried to offer opportunities for the radical milieu (not just single groups, but multiple overlapping activist circles) to meet and talk about broad issues and ideas, which also allowed some of the issues that lead to burnout (judgemental atmospheres, oppressive behaviour, unequal labour) to be brought into the open – though certainly not solved!

Along the bottom axis of our square (2c) is the synthesis of 'not-success' and 'not-failure', which we have identified as 'culture'. This is, to the best of our understanding, the near constant state of social movements. Because the horizon of social movement potential exceeds the limited and stated forms of 'success', often articulated as the concrete goals of

struggle or specific campaign objectives, the work of movements is never done. This dwelling between 'not-failure'
and 'not-success' represents the key psychosocial landscape
of social movement actors. Amidst this, it is the ability to
keep hope, solidarity and purpose alive, for both groups and
individuals, that is the heart of social movement energies.
We might call the horizon of social justice at the 'top' of
the square (2a) the terrain of 'transcendence', the necessary
wish for a different society that animates radicalism. The
antithetical 'bottom' (2c) is the terrain of 'immanence', the
everyday, existential shared landscape of perseverance. It is
between these two that the 'radical imagination' exists: it is
not only the ability to dream of different worlds, it is the
ability to live between those worlds and this one, between
'not-success' and 'not-failure'.

Our research partners in Halifax developed many ways of
doing this. Most reported that relationships were key. Many
talked about needing to keep spheres and areas of life separate
from their activism, or maintain other groups of friends and
hobbies. Many of our participants' abilities to dwell between
not-success and not-failure were cast in reference to history,
to the way that movements in the past appeared to be 'going
nowhere' until, all of a sudden, there was a breakthrough.
Interestingly, perhaps the most pervasive technique for dwelling
in this space was a cynical, wry knowingness, often articulated
as a sardonic fatalism. Often with reference to the worsening
global ecological situation and the consolidation of corporate
and state power, almost all our participants adopted a sort of
cagey and resigned tone towards their seemingly Sisyphean
labours, which perhaps helped insulate them from the heartsick

reality whose naked appearance might lead to demobilizing fury or despair.

We have called this axis (2c) 'culture' because it helps reveal the importance of stories, images, practices, beliefs, relationships, ideas and institutions that allow movements to persist (see Selbin 2010). It is this sense of culture (understood as a material and symbolic practice of meaning-making rather than merely as a thing one possesses) which allows us to see that movements do not exist in isolation. Almost everywhere, multiple movements enjoy overlapping 'membership' (whether formal or informal) and are cross-cut by a social commons constituted by relationships and individuals: sometimes colleagues, sometimes neighbours, sometimes lovers, sometimes rivals. Radical social movements, then, are both the products and the producers of culture at the crossroads of not-success and not-failure, an ecology of perseverance.

Our argument here is that the space between not-success and not-failure is a vital one for researchers to study and to reimagine as a zone of intervention. This is not only because it (rather than definitive success or failure) is the real substance of social movements, but also because it is in this hiatus – a beautiful word, which stems from the Latin word for 'opening' – that solidarity researchers might be able to find their place in relation to the social movements they study. What if, rather than 'helping movements succeed', we conceived of our role as supporting them to develop, refine and question strategies for dwelling between not-success and not-failure?

Returning now to the left-hand side of the square (2d), we can see how limited the simple contrast of social movement success and failure can be, which can only hope to measure these terms either by movements' own stated yardsticks or by rubrics imposed by the researcher from the outside. Movements do not 'succeed' or 'fail' except in the retrospective gaze of history. Rather, they exist in the interstice, in the hiatus. They are born of and driven by (often unstated, unarticulated) common dreams of a world beyond the binary of 'success' and 'failure'. They dwell in the everyday space of 'not-success' and 'not-failure'. From this perspective, successes are often worse than failures: when an electoral victory leads to demobilization, for instance, leaving participants scattered and lost. And, by the same token, failures can be better than successes. In both New York City and Halifax, the eviction of Occupy demonstrators (see Chapter 7) was a failure in the sense that the forces of the state rendered impossible the stated objective of the movement: to occupy public space. But out of the 'failures' in both contexts have emerged a plethora of new activist networks and groups working on a wide variety of issues, animated by the utopian horizon beyond success and failure and actuated by activist techniques for dwelling between not-success and not-failure (see Taylor 2013). This is to say nothing of the spectacle of their eviction by police, which illuminated the underlying political reality of state repression for countless witnesses. This is not to say successes are unimportant. Sometimes successes are simply successes, and failures merely failures. Successes often lead to greater levels of mobilization as people feel the momentum of victory. Failures often lead to burnout, if not prison terms or worse. Rather, we are arguing that when we pluralize our understanding of this binary, we gain a more profound insight into radical social movements and the spaces for solidarity research.

Solidarity research: dwelling in the hiatus

We can use the same framework to reinterpret the study of radical social movements. Let us begin by contrasting what are typically considered research 'successes' and 'failures'. For mainstream academics, the measure of success is the ability to collect and interpret reliable data. More cynically, it is the ability to 'get published'. Failure is ideally conceived of as a methodological mistake, a failure to accurately or reliably measure the social world. In practice, failure means collecting boring data: data that doesn't illuminate anything particularly 'new'.

We are less interested in this traditional research and more interested in that which attempts to find solidarity with movements. For those of us committed to this path, success and failure are more difficult to imagine. For some, success still means cultivating reliable data, often at the behest of movements themselves, or in order to illuminate and legitimate movements through the prestige of the academy (see Chapter 1). For others, success is to be measured by how well movements are served by the research, often by a standard the movements themselves determine. But in either case, as with the movements in the square above (p. 126), the researcher (p. 134) exists between an impossible utopian relationship with the movement, one of perfect reciprocity and immediacy (3a), and a reality of not-succeeding and not-failing (3c). Let us once again go through our four syntheses.

On the left-hand side we have the synthesis of solidarity research success and not-failure (3d). This means that, according to whatever criterion was imagined (whether the cultivation

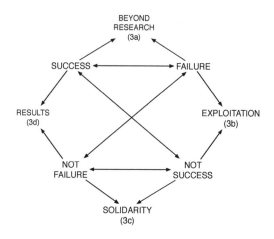

The expanded movement research square

of reliable data or service to the movement in question), the researcher has succeeded and avoided failure, in the sense that many of the pitfalls that accompany social movement research have been evaded: the exploitation or disruption of the researcher or research, the often corrosive effect of power and privilege differentials, the use of researcher information by law enforcement agents, or the alienation of the research from the movements, or from academe. This outcome is, of course, desirable for all sorts of noble reasons. The Jamesonian square method does not ask us to abandon the 'left hand' of the equation (3d), only to recognize that there is more to the picture.

Thus, on the right-hand side we can understand the antithesis of 'results' and the synthesis of 'failure' and 'not-success' as exploitation (3b). Beyond simply collecting uninteresting or unreliable data, this side of the researcher–social movement relationship can open onto forms of exploitation. Here exploitation might include the exploitation of the movement by the researcher, in the sense that the research serves the latter's career at the expense of the former. Or, vice versa, social movements may 'exploit' a willing researcher, either demanding all their time or placing limits on their autonomy, which restricts the odd (almost perverse) freedom and the critical element of 'play' that is in many ways unique to university-based researchers in an age where neoliberalism has dramatically confiscated almost all other forms of critical intellectual autonomy. Exploitation here refers to a failure of responsibility in the radical, poetic sense of the term: a failure for one party to be 'responsible' or 'responsive' to the other, to be 'accountable', in the sense of being able to 'give an account of oneself', to 'settle accounts' (Butler 2005: 9–21). In other words, the synthesis of 'failure' and 'not-success' (3b) is the perpetuation of power imbalances that undermine the research relationship. The synthesis of 'failure' and 'not-success' here speaks to the betrayal of the utopian vision (3a) that is at the heart of solidarity research.

And what of that vision? Just as social movements dream of something beyond their immediate goals, so too do solidarity researchers, we believe, dream of a utopian horizon. Like all horizons, this one recedes as we approach, and its contours are always hazy and incomplete. But, like out first square (p. 126), this utopian horizon is one where the original antinomy is reconciled, where research success and failure are no longer in opposition. This would be a world where the line between researcher and movement would no longer be tenable, where 'research' is folded back into the fabric of daily life, and where the unequal and unfair division of labour (where some are 're-searchers' and others are 'researched') disappears. Experiments in co-research have striven for this horizon and have often approached it in admirable ways (see Shukaitis, Graeber and Biddle 2007). But the true utopian horizon cannot be reached because, in a way, it would be a moment where research itself would be unnecessary. Just as radical social movements' utopian horizon is a world that has no use for social movements, the researcher's horizon renders the dreamer anachronistic. Solidarity researchers do the work they do because they think it is an important way of confronting injustice, beyond the 'normative' constellations of 'success' and 'failure'. In so doing, they dream a world beyond the sorts of injustice they believe research can help eliminate.

More practically, radical solidarity researchers develop methods and strategies that are always, even when pragmatic, grounded in the utopian belief that if the power imbalances of the researcher–researched relationship cannot be overcome (in this society), they can be worked through. And it is this 'working through' that we identify with the bottom quadrant of our square (3c), which we have identified as 'solidarity'. This is the state of 'not-success' and 'not-failure' familiar to us from the social movement square, and likewise it is the space of active waiting, of anticipatory pragmatics, of the pregnant hiatus. Researchers dwelling in this place navigate the ongoing difficulties, pitfalls and irreconcilable conundrums of working with social movements with an eye on the north star (the top of the square). As with social movements, this dwelling between success and failure is a practice of radical patience. And in that it is fundamentally at odds with the neoliberal university obsessed with 'results', research 'deliverables' and quantifiable baubles of knowledge.

Whither failurism?

Recently, political theorists including Jodi Dean (2012) and Wendy Brown (1999) have taken aim at what they characterize broadly as the left's obsession with failure as a melancholic attachment, one that sees social movements narcissistically devour themselves by fixating on small, largely insignificant gains rather than demanding and building to win meaningful social change. These theorists, frustrated by the 'soft' liberal anarchistic tendencies in radical movements (notably, Occupy Wall Street) call for a rejection of failurism and a return to what Dean calls 'the communist horizon'. While Dean is not exactly calling for a return to the rigid party organization and ideology of the twentieth century, she believes that left social movements need to embrace bold and broad visions of a communist society and eschew the sorts of liberal individualism and shortsightedness that produce morose and cannibalistic activist subcultures rather than thriving, powerful movements against capitalism.

Our vision of a research politics of not-success and not-failure is not unsympathetic to this objective. In claiming that social movements dwell in the hiatus, we are not necessarily celebrating that fact, although we do not believe movements will ever achieve some transcendent status of pure success. In fact, we believe that movements that are too triumphalist about their own narrative are extremely dangerous. We are also concerned that authors like Dean, in their justified impatience with leftist narcissism, might invite their readers to ignore the important anti-oppression work movements often do (including seemingly endless soul-searching and self-flagellation over themes of privilege, exclusion and inaccessibility along the axes of class, race, gender, education, citizenship status and cis/trans politics, among others). While often excruciating and time-consuming, this work cannot simply be reduced to liberal individualism and melancholic pathology.

If we were to imagine a move towards a research solidarity based on the framework of the hiatus illustrated above, it would not mean a glorification of failure. Such a move would, rather, allow researchers to reimagine their own role vis-à-vis the movements they work with and the impasses, limits, frustrations and contradictions they inevitably face. In our Radical Imagination Project, for instance, many of our partners reported that the interviews and dialogue sessions were a rare occasion for them to articulate and share – in an open-ended, reflexive and non-sectarian space – broader visions of what they were fighting for, and to be forced to link those visions to their current forms of activism. These solidaristic research interventions became a means to open up the productive tensions between success and failure. As Dean notes, the left's obsession with failure emerges in part from the way social movement cultures get caught up in the often mundane and unending nature of struggle. The methodological approach we are dreaming of here is one that sees the researcher help create a movement space for broader reflection and strategizing that, outside of more formal party structures, rarely exists. In this way, our proposal to imagine and work with movements as they dwell in the hiatus between not-success and not-failure is not a celebration of failurism. It may, in fact, help make movement beyond failurism possible.

Radical therapy

This approach intersects recent debates within activist circles about the place of self-care. Drawing on both the legacy of the feminist dictum that 'the personal is political' and the way non-white activists (and non-activists) have been forced to develop forms of individual and collective resilience against the psychological and physical toll of existence and struggle within a white-supremacist society, Audre Lorde (1988: 131) famously wrote that 'caring for myself is not self-indulgence, it is self-preservation and that is an act of political warfare.' Inspired by these words of wisdom and others, 'self-care' has become a key theme in recent movement dialogues, especially in anarchist, queer, trans, anti-racist and feminist struggles where the wages of survival within an oppressive system take their toll on the body, spirit and mind. Many of these discussions have sought to move beyond the archetype of the 'successful activist' discussed above and accept the reality that we are all wounded, imperfect, alienated subjects who bring to movements our partial, complex, confused and often painful histories and personal burdens. They have rejected the idea that movement participation needs to be an unending labour of self-sacrifice for future collective liberation and have generally promoted the building of movement cultures that make room for people to take breaks, to relax, to build relationships and to express frustration, hopelessness, pessimism and weakness in useful ways. Much of the impetus for a discussion of self-care has emerged from critical disabilities activism, and the recognition that common modes and expectation of movement participation exalt those who are not contending with physical or mental challenges. In these ways, the ideas and practices of self-care have challenged and expanded the idea of 'success' to encompass the mental, physical and spiritual health of activists, a move which has been supported, in the best cases, by a commitment to anti-oppression by which movements educate themselves to understand how their internal cultures and practices might be oppressive, exclusive or exploitative (for more on the complexities of anti-oppressive practice and politics, see Chapter 6).

These are nascent steps by which movements are coming to understand and embrace their role as spheres of radical social reproduction. Yet, along these lines, recent debates have highlighted the limits of the idea of 'self-care'. For Loewe (2012), writing in the online forum *Organizing Upgrade*, the language of self-care has become an almost fetishistic obsession within many movements, and one whose implications have become highly individualized. Loewe and others challenge us to imagine what effective forms of *community* care might look like that are built into movements seeking to be powerful forces of social change. For instance, care looks different for a single mother of three than it does for an unattached college student; it looks different for someone contending with clinical depression than it does for an undocumented activist under surveillance by border police. It also looks different when one accepts that movements are sites of and for struggle rather than places for individualized catharsis. Simply telling individuals to care for themselves better ignores the fact that many of us do not have the proper economic or social resources to do so, and the fact that the slings and arrows that wear us down are social and require social solutions.

Others have responded to this by noting that collective care is easier said than done and that, ultimately, individuals need to learn to identify for themselves the forms of healing that work for them. The debate continues to unfold, but one key dimension to all these discussions is the identification of capitalist alienation and the grinding effects of exploitation as fundamental barriers to organizing. This recognition also compels us to consider to what extent a new world can be crafted by subjects wrought of the current regime. Of course, this question is venerable, having emerged even from within the Frankfurt School and other Marxist theoretical orientations. But the problem takes on a new salience today and perhaps especially in the global North, where capital has a great deal invested in producing subjectivities and hierarchies, and where levels of alienation are perhaps most severe in the absence of more robust, rooted forms of collective identity and amidst the rampant commodification and financialization of life and social relationships.

Within this context, Italian autonomist activist and theorist Franco 'Bifo' Berardi (2009), predicts that

> Politics and therapy will be one and the same activity in the coming years. People will feel hopeless and depressed and panicky because they are unable to deal with the post-growth economy, and because they will miss their dissolving modern identity. Our cultural task will be attending to those people and taking care of their insanity, showing them the way to a happy adaptation. Our task will be the creation of social zones of human resistance that act like zones of therapeutic contagion. The development of autonomy is not totalizing or intended to destroy and abolish the past. Like psychoanalytic therapy it should be considered an unending process.

In other words, Berardi is arguing for a process of revolutionary transformation in the systematic and permanent failure of capital to make good on its promises of wealth, equality of opportunity and prosperity. Out of the psychic dissonance produced by a growing disconnection between individuals' fabricated hopes and aspirations, on the one hand, and the material circumstances of existence, on the other, a breach is opened that offers a possibility. Within such a system, the route out of capitalist social relations takes the form of a sort of radical therapy, helping individuals and groups 'treat' the 'insanity' that accrues to the material decomposition of the capitalist subject. While Berardi unfortunately overlooks the dramatically different costs and effects of this decomposition on different bodies (gendered, queer, disabled, racialized), his suggestion that politics – or, as he puts it, 'communism' – can be imagined as a form of never-ending therapy is useful. Not only does it recentre social relationships and care at the core of activism, it also avoids the triumphalism and hubris that have all too often accompanied Marxist narratives. While it risks contributing to narratives of failurism, the idea of radical activism as a form of eternal social, political and subjective therapy also opens up a space, in the present, for unrelenting revolutionary activity of dwelling in the hiatus. For Berardi, the creation of 'social zones of human resistance [and] therapeutic contagion' implies the building of everyday autonomy, solidarity and counter-power throughout society in ways that at once echo and go beyond more anarchistic and autonomist ideas of prefigurative politics and the building of tomorrow's social institutions and relationships within and against the present (Day 2005). Such an approach would see the building of movements as a conscientious and intentional act. In other terms, it would take seriously the strategic cultivation of movements as spaces of militant social reproduction.

Conclusion: beyond the middle-class imaginary

In this section, we have sought to demonstrate that the question of movement success and failure is fundamentally fraught, situated as it is at the intersection of socio-economic forces, personal biography, group structure and dynamics, and power relations. We have attempted to locate the problems our research participants and activists more widely face as part of struggles within and against a much broader crisis of social reproduction germane to neoliberal capitalism. And we have attempted to show how social movement researchers can reimagine their own responsibilities and potentialities in ways that take into account these challenges.

The radical imagination is, as we have argued, not an individual possession but a collective process, but this does not deny its personal, affective and biographical dimension. While the radical imagination may be a collective process, it is one activated and lived by individuals who come to that process with their own backgrounds and baggage, their own privilege, and their own cocktail of oppression.

Through our research and reflections, we would propose that the single most pressing challenge for the radical imagination, its single most powerful opponent now, is the potent and pernicious myth of middle-class success to which we have returned throughout this chapter. While there is of course nothing inherently wrong with the desire for material security and the safe and pleasurable reproduction of social life, striving for what is, by now, a practically non-existent ideal of middle-class security represents a massive barrier to the radical imagination and social movements in general. Further, once its hollowness and impossibility are revealed, it can become fertile ground for the cultivation of bitterness, cynicism and betrayal that feed fascist movements promising security and a return to 'greatness' through authoritarian terror directed at the most vulnerable and visibly different. This is not to say that those working in jobs that offer some modicum of security or that pay a living wage are inherently enemies of or immune to the radical imagination. But it is to say that the *seduction* of an individualistic middle-class escape from the crisis of social reproduction is fundamentally at odds with the ability to imagine and reproduce the world *otherwise*.

This is because the middle-class promise is one fundamentally predicated on the individualistic pursuit of social equilibrium, peace and security. While liberal thinkers might believe that the middle-class lifestyle is feasible for everyone, and that all that is required is a slightly more equal system of opportunities, we believe that this promise is impossible and undesirable. Not only has middle-class security always been bought with the displacement of the crisis of social reproduction onto others (women, the 'third world', racialized people, migrants, queer folk), it has never truly worked even for those within the so-called middle class. Middle-class belonging was the prize offered by capital for our obedience, docility and complicity, and as it turns out it has always been a ruse.

The radical imagination atrophies when politics is imagined as merely the extension of middle-class belonging to wider constituencies of people, whether they are local marginalized populations or globalized workers or women or refugees. Similarly, individuals lose their capacity to participate in the radical imagination to the extent that they embrace for themselves or their comrades the middle-class dream of an individualized escape from the crisis of social reproduction.

The key challenge the radical imagination now faces is this: we live in a time of two contradictory shifts. On the one hand, the promise of middle-class inclusion and individualized escape from the crisis of social reproduction is being sold to almost everyone. While in reality middle-class jobs and the security they promise still disproportionately accumulate to straight, white, able-bodied, cis-men, capitalism is in the process of grudgingly dismantling formal, legal barriers to this dream for those so long denied access to its pursuit: racialized people, women, queer and trans people, and other marginalized folks. This is not to deny the intense systemic, interpersonal and institutional barriers that remain (and must remain for the system to operate) to many marginalized people; it is only to say that the dream of middle-class inclusion, even if it is only realized by a tiny fraction of marginalized people, has been offered as a means to co-opt and corrupt struggles for equality and social justice.

But, on the other hand, middle-class existence is increasingly materially impossible. Those members of the so-called middle class are not insulated from the crisis of social reproduction, though they may feel its impacts less intensely, less violently and less destructively than those of us who are socially or economically marginalized. We are amidst a political situation where those who have struggled and competed to earn a place in the middle class are finding themselves denied the sorts of security, prosperity and happiness they were led to expect.

To the extent that capitalism is seen to plausibly offer access to middle-class security, it is unlikely that radical Northern social movements will obtain the sorts of social change they seek. It is not enough for movements to simply decry, mock and offend middle-class sensibilities and habits. Those goods and hopes that the myth of middle-class belonging promises are not in and of themselves unworthy: the right to enjoy peace, security, family (broadly imagined), friendship, education, creativity, time off, and meaningful relationships. The key for movements going forward will be providing similar or better goods and hopes to their own members, as well as to those whom they hope to convince and recruit. Whether they are movements that build alternative structures of social reproduction in the here and now (cooperative housing projects, local food initiatives, day-care collectives, etc.) or promise them in the post-capitalist future, the single most pressing barrier to the radical imagination is the belief that escape from the crisis of social reproduction can be achieved at the level of the individual.

PART THREE

Making space, making time

FIVE

The life and times
of radical movements

The perpetuity of oppression within struggles for social justice and liberation may seem like a contradiction, yet it is all too common. During the course of the Radical Imagination Project issues relating to structured oppressions both outside of and within the fabric of social justice movements were expressed by our participants with relative frequency. In the interview phase of our research and in the course of our three Dialogue sessions (see Chapter 2), as well as in casual conversations outside of formal research contexts, activists and organizers often raised the issue of racism, sexism, heteronormativity, homophobia and transphobia, classisim and ablism occurring within social justice movements more broadly. Our research participants did not simply decry oppression rhetorically, they wrestled with it in terms of situating it in relation to their understanding of the dominant system, the work of social change, the organization of social movements, and their own lives and work.

In this chapter and the next, we argue that there is a key fault line in social movements regarding the conflict between economic and social axes of power, or between capitalist *exploitation*, on the one hand, and *oppression* based on other systems of power, on the other. We explore this tension in terms of temporalities: shared ways of imagining time. In this chapter, we trace the development of a certain approach to the times of social movements through the twentieth century and highlight the importance of shared movement temporalities. In the next chapter, we take up the perpetuation of oppression within social movements and suggest that the desire to 'make space' for difference within movements, while often well intentioned, is not sufficient to answer the challenges of oppression and struggle in an oppressive society. Rather, we suggest a shift away from 'making space' and towards 'making time', arguing that the time taken to confront and overcome oppression fundamentally transforms movement temporalities, and for the better.

Anne Bishop (2002: 51) defines oppression as the act of one group exercising power over another in order to maintain structured injustice and inequality at the expense of the latter and to the benefit and privilege of the former. Yet, by Bishop's own admission, oppression leaks out of strict definitions, just as it seeps into everyday life, relationships, subjectivities, expectations and, we would highlight, the imagination. This is true both of those who endure oppression and of those who (wittingly or unwittingly) exercise oppression over others or benefit from an oppressive society – and, to make matters more complicated, these are not mutually exclusive: those who suffer oppression are not immune from oppressing others. While it certainly characterizes social life writ large in capitalistic societies, oppression is by no means limited to our current socio-economic order. Neither is oppression limited to only mainstream or hegemonic socio-political and economic relations and institutions. In fact, oppression can and often does inhabit those formations – such as social movements – avowedly or allegedly fashioned to confront and abolish it.

But, aside from these fairly standard observations, what is the relationship between oppression and forms of structured inequality and injustice (notably capitalism)? Are they co-extensive? Are they complementary but mutually exclusive? Does a system of structured inequality and exploitation like capitalism have to be abolished before systematic oppressions based on gender, age, ability, race, sexuality and more are addressed? Is the reverse the case? Is oppression the same as identity politics? Is class the central axis of a genuinely revolutionary struggle for liberation? Does a focus on oppressions obscure a critical analysis of the material basis of structured violence, exploitation and injustice? Does a denial of the significance of oppression – both in society at large and within the space of movements themselves – fundamentally undermine a movement's radically transformative capacity? Is (as some of our interviewees suggested) anti-oppressive politics a Trojan Horse for liberalism and a bourgeois self-help ethic? Or does (as others insisted) fixating on the material inequality and structured exploitation of capitalism to the exclusion of (or in preference to) racism, sexism, colonialism, and so on, simply reproduce oppressive structures? Situating, unpacking and critically grappling with the relationship between oppression and exploitation lay at the heart of many of our participants' attempts to conceptualize and articulate a genuinely radical social justice practice. Yet, in reality, many of the (interpersonal, social, economic, discursive and actual) violences made possible by oppressive relationships were reproduced in the course of their activism. Indeed, in a telling moment during the course of the project, the tensions and contradictions surrounding the articulation of a political ethic capable of addressing systemic inequality and injustice were startlingly revealed.

During the second Dialogue session, titled '(anti-)Capitalism and the Struggle against Oppression', held in April 2011 in a black box of a room at the back of the Bus Stop Theatre in Halifax, three research participants with considerable histories in social justice activism initiated a facilitated discussion focusing on the relationship between struggles against capitalism and struggles against oppressions. Each speaker – two women and one man (one a racialized person, one a movement elder) – spoke for between five and fifteen minutes, reflecting on their own histories of activism and revealing something about struggles against exploitation and oppression. While each speaker offered powerful and poignant insights on the long haul of struggle for social justice, the way capitalism requires and nurtures oppressions, and the necessity for rigorous awareness of the replication of oppression within the fabric of movements, one speaker's personal reflections were particularly powerful. Narrating her history in anti-racist, anti-poverty and direct-action activism, she told a story about her own experience of sexual violence at the hands of a male activist. She then proceeded to illuminate the ways in which radical movement spaces and practices, as well as the broader culture of activism, actually facilitate this kind of predatory behaviour and ultimately protect the perpetrators from any real consequence of their actions. Her narrative was eloquent, powerful, unapologetic and unequivocal and seemed to demand that those in attendance – some thirty social justice radicals and other members of the public – engage these issues openly.

Yet, while another young woman in attendance sought to engage the issue of rape and wondered why the focus in social justice movements was not simply to demand that men not rape and how that objective might be achieved, she was followed by a host of young male activists in the room who subsequently managed to turn the focus towards a general and highly idealized discussion of the concept of solidarity and the abstract principles of social justice struggle. Despite our attempts as facilitators to reorient the discussion towards the concrete intersections of structured oppressions and structured exploitation, its overall trajectory arced far out into a sea of speculative and theoretical interventions, many of which seemed to exhort those in attendance not to sow internal divisions within movements by advancing their own issues and interests.

In essence, the Dialogue session became a microcosm of the larger dynamics that, according to many activists, allow for oppressions to be perpetuated within movement spaces in systematic and deeply pernicious ways. A concrete, critical engagement with oppression was (perhaps unintentionally but no less problematically) denied in favour of a highly abstracted and intellectualized discussion of politics that became dominated by many of the young white male activists in attendance. Without attributing too much significance to a single event in the course of one research project, the dynamic witnessed at this second Dialogue session is not at all out of step with those described over the past several decades by activists raising issues relating to the reproduction of oppressions within avowedly radical milieus. Rhetorical affirmation of a commitment to anti-oppressive practice is frequent; its realization in the living practices of activists and organizers is much less so. The ways structural oppressions can occlude and pollute the radical imagination and radical political practice, and what those engaged in social justice struggle can do to confront and dismantle them, are the focus of these two chapters.

In this chapter we examine the histories of radical social justice struggle in the north of the Americas in order to discover the temporal politics of the tension between (economic) exploitation and (cultural) oppression. We suggest that in each moment of struggle a particular politics of time has been active, one that encourages and renders urgent certain tactics, strategies and priorities – often with the effect of sidelining or marginalizing the struggle against oppression. In the next chapter we engage with a diverse group of activists and scholars who have analytically and theoretically grappled with oppression and its relation to structured exploitation and inequality. Readers looking for any easy or conclusive answers to these vexing problems will be disappointed. In this chapter and the next we merely hope to lay out some resources for thinking with the problem.

Our suggestion here is that, while all too often social movements pay lip service to the idea of *creating space* for 'diversity', this rhetoric often comes at the expense of *creating time* for the unending work of building solidarity and anti-oppression. Among radical movements, the notion that anti-oppressive politics take 'too much' time, or that there is some greater urgency that trumps dealing with oppression, is all too common. In Chapter 6 we argue that anti-oppressive work is important not merely because it has the potential to actualize the liberal ideals of pluralism, diversity, multiculturalism and inclusion. That is, these politics do not merely transform the spaces of movements.

In recognizing that the politics of anti-oppression constitute an unending challenge to the forms of learned, habituated and reproduced privilege and power, the radical imagination evolves beyond a liberal idealism which, in the end, merely reinforces reigning structures of oppression.

The co-optation of radicalism in the anglophone North Atlantic

Debates over the central axes, terrains and subjects of radical struggle have been and continue to be an enduring feature of left organizing. This claim is undoubtedly true in any given location but it has certainly characterized radical struggles for social justice in the anglophone North Atlantic world over the last century. While a commitment to direct action and an understanding of struggle expanded to encompass the whole of the lifeworld, rather than just sites of capitalist accumulation, are often linked to the rise of the New Left in the 1960s and its radical descendants in the 1970s and 1980s, this radicalized political praxis harks back at least to the work of pacifists and labour activists in the early part of the twentieth century (Polletta 2002: 27–8). In the USA, radical pacifists were key to the Civil Rights Movement, helping to found the Congress of Racial Equality (CORE), the Southern Christian Leadership Conference (SCLC), the Fellowship of Reconciliation (FOR), and train leaders like Martin Luther King Jr in non-violent resistance, as well as assisting in the organization of freedom rides through the deep South (Epstein 1991: 29; Polletta 2002: 27). In both the USA and Canada, pacifists not only argued for a political utopianism that refused to withdraw from the world but were also openly critical of the social structures and cultures that sustained militarism (Epstein 1991: 28; Polletta 2002: 27; Neigh 2012). Prefiguring the New Left by decades, pacifists joined the commitment to democratic practice within movements to strategies of mass, non-violent direct action. At the same time, they critiqued both the technocratic tendency of Western capitalism and the economic reductionism of orthodox Marxism, while highlighting the centrality of the struggles of racialized people and of international solidarity (Polletta 2002: 27; Neigh 2012). While radical pacifism would not ultimately form the animating core of radicalized social justice struggles either in the USA or in Canada after the mid-twentieth century, its legacy would inform future generations of radicals in enduring and important ways.

From one angle, the legacy of these struggles was a new focus on the *times* of activism. On the one hand, the pacifist influence (in spite of religious undertones) avoided a temporality based on the sudden and total revolutionary transformation of society, a notion that had held sway in radical movements since the late eighteenth century with its iconic revolutions. Instead, revolutionary change was seen as a slower process by which social life, individual subjects and economic relationships could be transformed. While revolutionary outbursts might be an important part of this process, the dismal example of the Soviet Union (especially in the wake of the invasion of Hungary and the repression of protesters there in 1956) disabused many on the radical left of the belief that a top-down, total revolution would magically eliminate oppression, power and domination in society. The pacifist movement also highlighted the idea that one needed to take time to 'work on oneself'. They understood war and violence as not merely the acts of states but rooted in the responses, ideas, habits and behaviours of individuals. This meant that movements began to prioritize a certain understanding of the revolutionary subject as a project of self-making, as a work of introspection and transformation that took time. While the cultivation of a charismatic revolutionary/intellectual persona (e.g. Lenin, Gramsci, Guevara, etc.) had pre-dated this, the notion that the revolutionary change depended on the transformation of each individual introduced a new rhythm into the radical imagination.

In the USA and Canada, the twentieth century witnessed the co-optation of the organized labour movement by the most privileged sectors of the industrial working class, leading to the preeminence of a form of a business unionism that sought to secure a 'seat at the table' for these sectors with power-holders and a larger share of the profits of industrial capitalism. Substituting a managerial technocratic approach for organizing and action, business unionism largely abandoned the most vulnerable sectors of the working class – including women, racialized people and precarious workers – while simultaneously working to prop up the dominant order rather than challenging the systems of oppression and exploitation at its core. But business unionism and the organizations which came to embody it were by no means exhaustive of what organized labour struggle in the spirit of social justice could contribute or achieve. In the USA, outside of the conservativism of the American Federation of Labor, dissident union strains enacted a politics based on the belief that a truly democratic pedagogy could be a force to catalyse movements for radical social change (Polletta 2002: 24). In the 1920s, they realized this commitment through a proliferation of union education programmes, independent labour colleges and university-affiliated summer schools. While these initiatives would not survive the attacks against them – coming from both the right in the form of anti-communist repression and the left via sectarianism and infighting – they would nevertheless serve to train and inspire generations of labour, pacifist and civil rights activists, shaping radical politics in the United States for decades to come (Polletta 2002: 35–6).

The terrain of radical politics was also fractured by divisions between white radicals born in the USA and those who were more recent immigrants (Epstein 1991: 27). The former tended to be relatively privileged, at least from the perspective of social capital, coming as they often did from the ranks of the self-employed, farmers and skilled workers and with a politics that tended towards populism, democratic reformism, spirituality and even utopianism (Epstein 1991: 27). Radicals who had emigrated more recently were drawn more often from the ranks of the emerging industrial working class with a politics much more oriented to class, pragmatic questions of materiality and distribution, and steeped in Marxism and other socialist traditions (Epstein 1991: 27). Notwithstanding radical experiments in forging solidarity across lines of difference such as the Industrial Workers of the World (IWW), the mainstream labour movement in anglophone North America tended to abandon those most in need of it in favour of advancing the interests of the most privileged members of the working class. This was also due, in no small part, to waves of private and state-backed terror unleashed against militant and radical labour organizers. In the first half of the twentieth century, the murder of IWW and other organizers, especially when they sought to undermine the colour line and mobilize white and non-white workers, was a common practice (Buhle and Schulman 2005). After the Second World War, anti-communist sentiment, policy and harassment, which culminated in the infamous 'witch trials' orchestrated by Senator Joseph McCarthy in the 1950s, effectively vanquished radicalism and militancy in the American labour movement.

In Canada, organized labour would similarly follow a trajectory leading from organizing and agitation to compromise, technocratic management and atrophy, born of an uncritical commitment to mainstream electoral politics. While dissident union strains such as the IWW engaged in committed and explicitly revolutionary organizing and action in the 1930s, these radical trajectories would ultimately be eclipsed by the business unionism embodied by the Canadian Labour Congress (CLC) (McKay 2005: 156). Wandering far afield from a commitment to recognizing the intersectionality of systemic oppressions and their role in maintaining structured exploitation under capitalism and its political trappings of liberal democracy, the CLC would, in the 1960s, align closely with the Co-operative Commonwealth Federation (CCF) to form the liberal leftist New Democratic Party (NDP) (McKay 2005: 173–4; Warnock 2005:82). Rather than empowering the struggle of organized labour against capitalist exploitation and its structured oppressions, the formation of the NDP and the wedding of organized labour to mainstream electoral politics would serve rather to discipline the labour movement in the hope, however faint, of electoral success at provincial and federal levels.

In the 1920s and 1930s, the Communist Party in Canada and the USA made important contributions to a radical politics concerned with oppressions and not just class-based exploitation. In step with the Communist International and its prediction that the collapse of capitalism was imminent, the Communist Party in both countries sought to build revolutionary organizations while refusing to cooperate with liberals and socialists, a militant stance which appealed to many marginalized and oppressed groups, including the unemployed and some racialized communities (Epstein 1991: 24–5; McKay 2005: 158–9). Following Roosevelt's New Deal in the USA, the adoption of similar Keynesian measures aimed at 'national economic and social management' in Canada, and the failure of attempted socialist revolutions elsewhere, however, the avowedly radical stance of the Party in both countries quickly gave way to an accommodationist one predicated on industrial organizing, winning a seat at the table for the labour movement, expanding the welfare state, and generally seeking greater legitimacy for the industrial working class in the eyes of mainstream society (Epstein 1991: 25; McKay 2005: 160). This retreat from an explicitly radical stance fundamentally undermined the Party's base, especially in the most marginalized and oppressed sectors. While the Communist Party in both the USA and Canada has been credited with 'feeding ideas' to the labour movement and the Keynesian welfare state, as well as promoting a vision of society as multi-ethnic and multiracial, the move from an explicitly revolutionary politics to a reformist orientation, ultimately consigning them to marginality (Epstein 1991: 26).

Here, the dream of a revolutionary Marxism based on the building of the class consciousness necessary to generate the political momentum to seize state power was replaced with another, more quietist and gradualist, temporality. Marxism had always been animated, in part, by the notion that only in a worker-directed society could modernist progress advance unimpeded. Capitalism was to be grudgingly admired for its ruthless 'creative destruction' of outmoded social norms, technologies, and social structures and institutions, but reviled for the way it alienated and perverted the power of the working class and so unequally distributed the rewards of 'progress'. While this narrative located class tensions and struggle at its heart, it was not incompatible with the temporality of liberal democracy, which likewise shared a faith in the humanist project of the Enlightenment that saw Western society as breaking free of the shackles of history and ever marching towards (sometimes ruthless and ruinous, but ultimately beneficial) social and technological innovation. By the post-war moment, trade unions and socialist parties found that their integration into mainstream politics could be justified by the promise that cooperation with the capitalist welfare state would see capitalism share more equally the spoils of progress. The 'post-war compromise' between labour and capital was based on the promise that a more acquiescent working class would (to a limited extent) enjoy a greater share of the prosperity to be generated by rising levels of productivity and technological advance. In other words, the modernist temporality of orthodox or 'scientific' Marxism, which underscored the ideological orientation of communist parties and many trade unions, 'created its own grave-digger', which allowed the working class to be conscripted to capitalist-nationalist temporality in the latter half of the twentieth century.

Notably, this temporality carried within an implicit understanding of oppression and society. In the liberal-democratic world-view, centred as it is around individualism and the mythology of equality of opportunity, oppressive behaviours and dynamics are, ultimately, the residual effect of outmoded prejudices and ignorance. Allegedly, as liberal institutions expand, the rule of law and constitutional rights will eliminate all legal and institutional barriers to the civic participation of traditionally oppressed people. What residual irrational prejudice remains can be solved through education or the pathologization of individuals. Accordingly, the struggle against oppression is one based on trust in the inherent benevolence and progressiveness of the capitalist system, joined to (often self-congratulatory) personal politics of acceptance, tolerance and open-mindedness for those with privilege, and persever-ance, patience and entrepreneurialism for those without. Within this temporality, the reigning structures and institutions of society, and especially the market, bear no responsibility for the continued existence of oppression. Rather, its persistence is the fault of noxious and primitive individual prejudices, often associated with the 'uneducated' working class, who 'don't know any better'. Worse still, labouring under the false belief that oppression is well on its way to being ended and that it has no systemic basis, this temporality insists that the struggles against sexism, racism and homophobia (among others) are now over, or simply a matter of cleaning up after the battle has been fought. This, in turn, gives way to a growing resentment among those with privilege towards those who dare to point out that these oppressions still do exist and, in fact, are in many ways worsening – evidenced, for example, by the rates of incarceration of black youth in the United States (Alexander 2010) and the horrifying statistics on sexual assault against women (National Intimate Partner and Sexual Violence Survey 2011). This toxic climate breeds a pernicious politics of backlash, in which anti-oppression activists and advocates are accused of practicing 'reverse racism' or 'reverse sexism' and are even lambasted as retrograde elements in an otherwise progressive system (see McCready 2013). As we shall see, this worldview continues to animate activist imaginaries, even among allegedly anti-capitalist and other radical movements.

By the 1950s, in the wake of the collapse of the Communist Party, the business unionism of big labour and post-war New Deal prosperity seriously diminished the prospects for the institutional left in the USA. In Canada, the demise of the Communist Party and the eclipsing of radical labour organizing by the CLC ushered in an era where systematic oppressions were understood as 'social problems' to be managed by a technocratic, nominally social-democratic state (McBride 2005: 29). What cannot be overstated is the significance of the substitution of amorphous commitments to social-democratic governance in place of a politics and analysis that understand systems of exploitation and the structured oppressions upon which they rest as the targets of genuine radical and revolutionary action. In this period many progressive actors in Canada and the USA turned away from a politics focused on abolishing capitalism and towards one predicated on the extension of bourgeois freedoms underwritten by liberal notions of social cohesion and order, good governance and a modicum of wealth redistribution. All these objectives orbited around the central figure of the Keynesian welfare state and its exalted subject, the white male middle-class individual consumer. This had two intertwined consequences. First, the stage was set for the rise of neoliberalism and the incredible social violence it would unleash; capital clearly had no intention of maintaining its end of the post-war compromise. Second, by investing in a liberalized political horizon that miscast fundamental social violences as 'problems' to be managed through policy, programmes, and ultimately the state's coercive and disciplinary power, the institutional left effectively abandoned any commitment to a serious politics of social justice, choosing instead to carve out a bigger piece of the pie for its privileged core.

In the post-war temporality, progress became less a narrative of social and collective liberation and more an individualized story of personal uplift. The personal aspirations of the newly minted middle class – to own a home and a car, to send one's children to university, to retire to a life of ease (see Chapter 4) – came to replace the more militant collective working-class dreams of ages past which focused more on the liberation of society from the shackles of the profit motive. The time of struggles ceased to be centred around building solidarity and common cause and more around the attempts of individual workers to gain comfort and wealth. Unions and social-democratic parties increasingly oriented their efforts towards supporting workers in these efforts, shying away from positions that noisily demanded a meaningful redistribution of wealth and adopting instead the liberal rhetoric of 'equality of opportunity'. It should, of course, also be noted that the post-war compromise only allowed for the middle-class integration of a very small section of the working class, namely white, straight, male workers, largely of Western European descent. The vast majority of workers of colour remained trapped in low-paying jobs or in the informal economy; women remained second-class political and economic citizens, providing not only formal labour at a fraction of the cost but also unpaid domestic labour; and the capitalist system in North America relied, as always, on the exploitation of immigrants and on neocolonial relationships around the world.

The rise and fall of the New Left

In many ways, the New Left that would emerge around the world in the 1960s and after was a consequence of a new generation of activists and organizers reacting to the moribund nature of the institutional left. Arguing that the New Left needs to be properly understood as a 'world-historical movement', George Katsiaficas identifies what he regards as its five key characteristics: opposition to racial, political and patriarchal domination as well as economic exploitation; a notion of freedom that extended beyond material deprivation to the production of subjectivities; a deepened and radicalized understanding of democracy; an enlarged conceptualization of revolution, emphasizing the socio-cultural as well as the politico-economic; and a tactical focus on direct-action tactics (1987: 23–7). While the lived reality of New Left struggles in countries around the world often did not live up to the promise of these principles – including, troublingly, its all-too-frequent inability to confront within its own spaces and structures the forms of exploitation and oppression it denounced without – it nevertheless provoked radical shifts in the conceptualization and practice of radical politics and alternative-building.

In the United States, the Civil Rights sit-ins that swept the South at the beginning of the 1960s heralded a new kind of politics that appealed powerfully to a younger generation, embodying the conviction that '[p]rotest in the service of high ideals, and enacted with love and mutual respect, could be militant, radical – and effective' (Epstein 1991: 48). Set against the backdrop of an older left characterized by 'political paranoia', 'internecine squabbling' and 'ineffectuality', a new radical political horizon emerged marked by an expansion of the terrain of struggle, a renewed commitment to direct action and democracy, and a recovery of an understanding of the mutually constitutive nature of exploitation and oppression (Polletta 2002: 123). Organizations like the Students for a Democratic Society (SDS) and the Southern Non-violent Coordinating Committee (SNCC) came out of this confluence as paragons of a new kind of politics focused not simply on issues of material inequality and injustice issues but on the socio-cultural, economic and political structures that reproduced the dominant order. The 1960s and 1970s also witnessed the emergence of New Left politics and struggles in the Canadian context. Organizations such as the Student Union for Peace Action, the Student Christian Movement and the Canadian Union of Students represented new forms of struggle increasingly driven by youth and with an emphasis on radical and decentralized action (McKay 2005: 184). Finding its centre in Montreal, Quebec, this New Leftism crystallized in relation to the Québécois struggle for independence from the Canadian state (McKay 2005: 186). Fusing international anti-colonial and anti-imperialist struggles with their own nationalist struggle against Canadian anglophone hegemony, embodied most militantly by the Front de Libération du Québec, Québécois leftists explicitly situated themselves as part of a world revolutionary process that was anti-capitalist, anti-imperialist and radical rather than liberal (McKay 2005: 187–8), even though this movement was itself often highly racist and colonial in its approach to non-white Quebécois and Indigenous peoples.

On both sides of the 49th parallel the temporality of the New Left was one that sought all too often to make a clean break with the past. In France this was emblematized by the idea that the young people who waged battles with police in the streets of Paris in May 1968 were a 'generation of orphans' (Ross 2002). The New Left rejected the hegemonic temporality of liberal capitalism, which saw a quietist labour movement conscripted into the service of a capitalist-led 'progress'; one that fed on brutal wars in the third world, oppression and exploitation at home, and depended on and fostered a deeply conservative cultural milieu. At the same time, the New Left also rejected what it saw as the complicit, or at least ineffective, temporalities of the 'Old Left', dedicated as they were to the much more gradual path to revolutionary change, including integration into the electoral sphere. The temporality of the New Left was one that sought to heighten the contradictions and tensions endemic to Western capitalist society. In the words of the Students for a Democratic Society and later the Weather Underground, it sought to 'bring the war home'. Newer Marxist paradigms including Maoism, Trotskyism and a renewed interest in Marxism–Leninism afforded this generation a way to break from older, seemingly ineffective leftist narratives and embrace a sense of historical immediacy and urgency. Testimonies of activists from the time reveal a sense of the immanence of revolution, the feeling that things not only could change dramatically and immediately, but were changing (see Haiven 2011b; Ross 2002). This often led to a preference for militant tactics of disruption and creativity (ranging from office occupations to combative street demonstrations to direct action against icons of capitalist power), usually to the exclusion of a focus on long-term organizing, political education, grassroots solidarity-building, or other 'slower' temporalities of resistance.

While New Left struggles teetered on the brink of revolutionary moments – evidenced by the militancy of 1968 – they would not realize this promise, and by the 1970s the radicalism and possibility associated with this cycle of struggle had largely dissipated. While many commentators explain this demobilization as due to a turn towards an explicitly revolutionary focus and the embracing of violence, others have suggested a more nuanced reading of this decline. In this reading, the decline of the New Left has been attributed to a failure by participants to link broader political and ideological arguments to more local particular sites of struggle and to their misreading of the dominant order's capacity for repression. Significantly, this decline is also linked to the New Left's inability to overcome internal divisions and its problematic tendency to reproduce oppression (notably patriarchy) within movement spaces (Epstein 1991; Katsiaficas 1987; McKay 2005; Polletta 2002). To this we might add that these movements all too often fetishized their temporality and its urging towards immediacy, urgency and presentness, and failed to 'make time' to deal with long-term planning, the longevity and the cunning of oppression. Nor did it attend to the (sometimes terrible) toll that this rhythm of radicalism would have on the minds, bodies, relationships, souls and identities of activists and organizers (see Passerini 1996).

The radical impetus of the New Left lived on through the 1970s and 1980s in the north of the Americas and elsewhere in movements oriented around do-it-yourself and squatting counterculture, direct action, environmentalism, anti-3 and anti-nuclear proliferation, and the liberation struggles of queer and racialized peoples (Epstein 1991; Katsiaficas 2006; McKay 2005; Polletta 2002). All these struggles, in different ways and with varying degrees of success, seek to address the legacy of left failure to address structural oppression within movement spaces themselves and to create the time to work through the hard questions of solidarity.

In this regard, no movement would be more important than radical feminism. In the 1960s vigorous critiques emerged of patriarchy, liberalism, capitalism and the failures of New Left organizations and the movement in general to address issues of male power and privilege, socialist and radical feminists would have a profound effect upon the social and political landscape within and outside of movements (McKay 2005: 192–5; Rebick 2005). Advancing a broad and multi-pronged struggle for women's liberation in economic, political and socio-cultural spheres, radical and socialist feminists profoundly affected the shape, ethic and practice of radical social justice struggle today (Graeber 2009; Katsiaficas 2006; McKay 2005; Polletta 2002).

In fact, practices of radical and direct democratic politics, as well as the insistence on addressing intersecting oppressions within the spaces of social movements, which have become hallmarks of the waves of radial social justice activism since the

1990s and beyond, owe their origin, in large part, to the work of radical and socialist feminists (Maeckelbergh 2009; Polletta 2002; Sitrin 2012). Indeed, it is no exaggeration to state that the alter-globalization movement as it was constituted in the north of the Americas would not have taken the shape that it did, nor arguably would it have achieved the resonance and significance it did, without the work of radical and socialist feminists. Of particular note is their critical work in coalition-building, foregrounding the intersectionality of oppressions and their integral relation to supporting exploitation, unsettling the notion of a single privileged subject of revolutionary struggle, and countering economically deterministic analyses of the possibilities for resistance and alternative-building (Ayres 1998; Clarke and Canadian Centre for Policy Alternatives 1997; Huyer 2004; MacDonald 2002). While a broad anarchist tradition has received recognition for inspiring the anti-hierarchical, radically democratic spirit and practice of the alter-globalization movement and the more recent waves of activism that have followed it (Graeber 2002; 2009), this debt is in many ways much more directly and concretely owed to the work of radical feminists. Indeed, the forgetting of this debt is symptomatic of the devaluation of feminist contributions more generally, as well as the reproduction of oppression within social movements and their narratives.

As these very partial histories of leftist political action traced above demonstrate, New Left formations and imaginations emerge in response not only to the challenges and opportunities of the dominant order but also to what they perceive to be the failures and systemic complicity of their own predecessors and contemporaries. As Barbara Epstein asserts, too often movements have criticized each other without recognizing either their own historical situatedness or the fact that there can be no 'correct revolutionary practice' given that movements respond to different challenges at different times (1991: 22).

In very broad strokes, and with considerable generalization and omission, we might characterize radical struggle for social justice in the north of the Americas in the twentieth century as constituted by four waves, each of which possessed a particular temporality. The first, in the early decades of the 1900s, focused on radicalized education, propagandizing and grassroots agitation. The second, during the 1930s and 1940s, was characterized by an increasing emphasis on engagement with the state, scientific models of social change, and the creation of the welfare state. The third, coalescing in the years after World War II, was marked by a questioning of the centrality of the industrial working class to radical and revolutionary politics and the New Left turn towards issues of race, gender, sexuality and the constitution of daily life. The fourth, beginning in the late 1970s and continuing through to the present moment, has been shaped by a focus on direct action, the significance of cultural and not just economic interventions, and a disavowal of the seizure of the state or a desire to exercise 'power over' as the central axis of revolutionary and radical struggle in favour of a multitude of resistances and alternatives in pursuit of a world, as the Zapatistas have asserted, in which many worlds can fit.

Each of these waves has not only responded to the challenges and opportunities perceived by those who constitute it in their own spaces and places, but has also embodied an understanding of what the terms, terrain and trajectory of social change struggle need to be. In offering that vision and materializing practice, each iteration of radical social justice struggle crystallizes around a certain set of answers to the question 'what is to be done' in relation to the time, space and material conditions in which action occurs. The living fabric of social movement organization and struggle reflects deeper understandings – tacit or explicit – of what constitutes the real goals and objectives of struggle, what oppressions and exploitations are most significant, how best to organize, how movements are sustained and how leadership is exercised, and more. But each of these phases is also animated by a tension around the question of time, timing and temporality. What is the objective of radical activism and organizing? A change in society? If so, when? Now? Soon? Eventually? Does this transformation rely on structural changes to laws, governments and institutions, or to subjects, identities and relationships? Should one objective be subordinate to the other? Is participatory democracy too slow? Is vanguardism too fast?

For this reason, and perhaps not surprisingly given that much social justice struggle emerges in the context of an urgent need to respond to some imminent injustice, movements often incubate and reproduce internally some of the very structured oppressions they rhetorically decry in wider society. All too often, struggles against oppressive systems that are the bedrock for exploitation are deferred, sacrificed at the altar of an idealized notion of revolutionary efficacy. And yet, as the exploration of anti-oppressive political practice and the cursory history of the waves of radical struggle in the north of the Americas offered above illuminate, the result of this sacrifice is not the realization of social justice but the replication of oppressions and ironically often the sabotage of mass-based struggles that could challenge the constituted order and the interests it serves.

The times of movement reproduction

Time and radical struggles for social justice and social change are deeply intertwined. Questions about strategies and tactics are frequently framed in relation to temporality and context. To restate the classic question: what is to be done and how are we to do it? What are the objective conditions here and now? Is this a revolutionary moment? How will we know? How are robust, formidable and durable movements for social change built? How much time will it take? How and to what will we commit ourselves? Notions of time are also implicated when activists consider structures of oppression and exploitation. The manner in which activists situate their understanding of the nature of radical and even revolutionary struggles is deeply embedded within often tacit understandings of how power is organized, what the nature of the dominant order is, and how oppressions and forms of exploitation are organized to sustain it. In the history of the modern left, this issue has frequently been framed in terms of class as an index of exploitation, against and perhaps above oppressions such as racism, sexism, homophobia, ageism, ableism and more. As Barbara Epstein notes with respect to the culture of protest and dissent in the United States, while it may be 'submerged' at times, '[c]ultural revolution, the transformation not just of economic or political structures but of the ideas that govern social life as a whole, has been a continuing theme in protest politics' (1991: 21). Ian McKay (2005) similarly asserts that the history of social justice struggles within the context of the Canadian state should be understood not simply as attempts at reforming or revolutionizing politico-economic relationships but as a series of experiments in 'living otherwise'. Indeed, as we have seen, while the 1960s are often celebrated as a time when movements – particularly those in the North Atlantic world – began to expand the terrain of struggle beyond the formally political and economic to include a focus on participatory democracy, direct action, subjectivity, the intersectionality of oppression, and the constitution of social life itself, these hallmarks of the New Left and the waves of radicalism that would follow it have much deeper roots (see Polletta 2002). In fact, scholars focusing on people's histories 'from below' have traced these threads through centuries of struggle against elite domination and exploitation during the making of the modern Atlantic world (Federici 2003; Linebaugh and Rediker 2000; Rediker 2004, 2007). The periodization of 'new' and 'old' lefts produces much more heat than light and in fact leads us politically and analytically away from the vital observation that radical struggles for social justice and social change have often understood the locus, form and process of confronting and transforming established systems of power, oppression and privilege in dynamic and expansive ways. The fact that specific movements have operated on the basis of a much more selective and restricted understanding of the nature of 'the problem' and the paths out of it does not diminish this.

Aside from questions relating to the way movements have sought to understand how systems of power are constituted and what the relationships between forms of exploitation, domination and oppression are, there stands another vexing problem that has received far less attention from both scholars and activists alike: the incubation and reproduction of these existing systems of oppression within social movements themselves. Importantly, this also intersects with a temporal axis. Addressing structural oppressions such as patriarchy and racism at the social level has been accorded differential levels of importance by activists and movements, depending in part upon the manner in which the nature of the dominant order and its attendant systems of power and privilege are understood. In other words, it's a question of priorities, of making time.

For example, in discussing why Marxist–Leninist parties have subordinated the struggle against patriarchy to struggles against imperialism and capitalism, Maria Mies explains that 'the independent mobilization and organization of women around the man–woman contradiction' has often been perceived to be 'a threat to the unity of the oppressed, the unity of the united front, and as inherently counter-revolutionary' because within the Marxist–Leninist conceptualization of revolution 'the "woman's question" constitutes a secondary contradiction which has to be tackled, ideologically, after the primary contradiction of imperialist and class relations have been solved' (1986: 198). Of course, prioritizing some power relationships over others in the context of radical or revolutionary struggle not only subordinates some to others, it also has the tendency to provide fruitful ground for such oppressions to root themselves in the soil of movements themselves. In other words, movement structures, spaces and practices can become incubators for a host of oppressive power relations rather than laboratories for experiments in liberation. Mies's analysis of how women's struggle for liberation is 'pushed back' after a successful struggle for national liberation in a Marxist–Leninist mode is, once again, insightful here. Even in moments where radical or revolutionary struggles are successful there is no single, totalizing threshold where everything simply changes and all oppressive or exploitative power relations are transformed into liberated, egalitarian ones. In the case of struggles for national liberation, Mies notes that because of the dominance of a basic model of growth and development on a world scale, even avowedly revolutionary movements can reproduce some of its core assumptions – for example, those relating to concepts of 'productive' and 'unproductive' labour (1986: 197). In this way, women's 'labour can ... be trapped in a process of ongoing primitive accumulation of capital which can then be fed into the building up of a modern economy and state' (1986: 197). Then there is the issue of subjectivity. So, while a revolution might make formal changes to the gendered division of labour in the context of struggle, such changes do not necessarily touch people's consciousness. As Mies explains, '[t]he fact that, after liberation, a national government has captured state power and that certain sectors of the economy have been socialized or are state-owned does not yet mean that all production relations have been revolutionized so that some sections of the people are not exploited for the benefit of other sections of the people' (1986: 198). In confronting one contradiction (capitalist exploitation) identified as 'primary' the national liberation struggle in a Marxist–Leninist mode thus ends up reproducing and entrenching other oppressions.

As we saw in Chapter 3, the Marxist-feminist approach to reproduction, developed by Mies and others, is extremely useful for the analysis of social movements. Movements are not only vehicles of political efficacy; they are interventions in the 'flows' and patterns of social reproduction at large, and they are also, at the same time (for better and for worse), alternative zones of social reproduction. They are, in a sense, always caught up in a contradiction between, on the one hand, seeking to be most efficacious in the transformation of social reproduction (through strategies that range from taking state power to merely influencing it, from building workplace insurgency to simply advocating a liberal notion of human rights) and, on the other, playing host to the human relationships, social dynamics, identities and subjectivities germane to the reproduction of social life. The value of the notion of reproduction is that it can draw our attention to this contradiction by shifting our attention from the spatial and organizational dynamics of movements (which has, by and large, been the predilection of social movement scholarship) and towards the temporal dimension of movement activity.

When we understand movements both as an intervention in the fabric of social reproduction at large and, at the same time, as constituted by their own alternative fabrics of reproduction, we can see a number of key points. The first is that social movements are interventions in time; they seek to transform the flow of events, the reproduction of society. The second is that movements themselves are less 'spaces' of politics than entities that comprise an approach to time, to how time is spent and valued. That is, when we see movements as spaces of reproduction, we sensitize ourselves to questions about what values, what norms, what ideas and what patterns are being reproduced, and what reproductive labour goes into their reproduction. We can understand the internal dynamics of movements as struggles over how the movement will be reproduced, and what sorts of norms, values, ideas, ideals, tendencies and power structures (formal and informal) are being reproduced. And we can ask the hard question of how those oppressive and unjust patterns of behaviour, and the privilege that flows from them, are not only reproduced in society at large (which movements may claim to be against) but also within movements themselves.

SIX

The temporalities of oppression

The reproduction of oppressive and exploitative power relations in the history of movement structures and struggles has been an important aspect of activist and scholarly analysis (see Epstein 1991; Polletta 2002). Of course, such reproduction is not simply a matter of historical interest. Michal Osterweil argues that part of the excitement generated by the alter-globalization movement was due to its embodiment and positing of deliberate reactions to the 'practical and theoretical failures of previous approaches of the Left', including the reproduction of systems of oppression within movements spaces themselves (2010: 82). Osterweil contends that these previous failures were not due to 'a thwarted strategy, a forced compromise or a political loss to another side' but were instead a result of 'fundamental problems with the modes and political visions these leftist movements were using and basing their practices on' (2010: 82). Such fundamental problems included: 'the reproduction of oppressions and micro-fascisms within supposedly progressive organizations'; an inability to deal with difference derived from 'contextual (historical, geographic, cultural, personal) specificities'; an inability to cultivate a meaningful and sustainable relationship between movements, everyday social realities and existing political forms and institutions; and, finally, a failure to relate radical and revolutionary movements to 'human desires – for leisure, love, fun and so on' (2010: 82–3). These perceived failures animated diverse attempts on the part of activists working beneath the alter-globalization banner to craft a new kind of political orientation and practice. Nevertheless, despite frequent and intentional references to feminism, feminist theory and the 'feminine', minoritarian, heterogeneous nature of the alter-globalization movement by participants – not infrequently by men – Osterweil contends that such invocations have rarely matched reality (2010: 83–4). Provocatively and incisively, she asks:

> What does it mean to see yourself as part of a movement governed by feminist and minoritarian logics when in so many of the most visible spaces, the voices and languages of women continue to be less audible? Does it matter if we have a fabulously astute and sensitive notion of what a good democratic – non-representative – politics would look like if we cannot involve more people in the conversation? Worse, is it of any use to have a great theoretical notion of the politics you want, but the very subjects you are claiming to be inspired by – that is those who have traditionally been othered, marginalised, excluded – are not present to participate in the discussion? If theoretical and reflective practice is so important to us today, even as an ethical and formal element, how do we live with such inconsistencies between our theoretical language and our experiences? (2010: 85)

Chandra Talpade Mohanty (2003) has articulated very similar concerns with respect to the relationship between the alter-globalization movement and feminism. Remarking upon what she perceives to be a parallel 'masculinization' of the discourses of capitalist globalization and anti-globalization movements, Mohanty notes that while class, race and nation figure fairly prominently in much anti-globalization analysis, 'racialized gender is still an unmarked category' (2003: 250). Despite the centrality of women and girls to globalized capitalism's labour regime, Mohanty notes the conspicuous absence of 'feminist analysis and strategies' in anti-globalization work, concluding that while 'feminists need to be anticapitalists ... antiglobalization activists and theorists also need to be feminists' (2003: 249). To understand the class-based exploitation unleashed by capitalism on a global scale is not enough, Mohanty argues, because it omits the vital axes of gender and race not only from the scope of critical analysis but also from the way resistance and alternatives are envisioned. Mohanty goes further, arguing that capitalist globalization's true violent, enclosing and exhausting nature is rendered most visible at one of the least visible social locations: racialized women living in the 'Two-Thirds World'. This means that these women, broadly defined, represent a particular epistemic community; their lived experience promises access to knowledge that surpasses that of privileged perspectives and can serve as the bedrock 'for envisioning transborder social and economic justice' (2003: 249–50). Mohanty charts a course for the feminist intervention she envisions, one capable of 'reimagining a liberatory politics' at the start of a new millennium: explicitly acknowledging and tracing the contributions of feminist political practice to the development of contemporary forms of social justice struggle; making the struggle for social justice as 'inclusive' as possible by anchoring our politics, analysis and theorizing in the lives and experiences of the most marginalized and obscured communities of racialized women in both 'affluent' and 'neocolonial' nations;

and advancing a feminist politics within movement ecologies in order to challenge many enduring patriarchal values, assumptions and practices (2003: 250). The path charted by Mohanty, while somewhat generalized, offers constructive and sensible signposts with which to navigate the dangers posed by the internalized reproduction of structures of oppression and exploitation within movement ecologies.

The invisibilization of those positioned most directly in the crosshairs of exploitation and oppression within even avowedly radical movements is not an aberrant occurrence; indeed, it characterizes too much of the spatiality and temporality of the radical left in the anglophone north Atlantic. As Elizabeth Betita Martínez (2000) asks – in what has become one of the most widely cited critiques of some of the most prominent privilege-blind practices of much of the alter-globalization movement in the global North – 'where was the color in Seattle?' Referencing the 30 November 1999 convergence in Seattle that was vital in shutting down the World Trade Organization ministerial meeting taking place in the city at the time, Martínez offers this question not merely rhetorically or to focus upon superficial notions of representation and identity. Instead, the title of her article and its content are an attempt to seriously engage with the consequences of racialized systems of privilege and oppression for social movements and for radical social justice politics. Martínez is optimistic that, if we actually take the time and have the courage to dwell with the messiness and the difficulty that emerge from these tensions, new horizons of common struggle will emerge.

At the same time, the deployment of grossly homogenizing categories as a route to exploring the profoundly conflicted terrain of radical politics and struggles for social justice can obscure at least as much as it is intended to reveal. Discussing the seemingly 'overwhelmingly white composition' of the alter-globalization movement as it constituted itself in the global North, activist and scholar A.K. Thompson notes that the relatively few accounts – Martínez's among them – that have actually taken up the nature of these 'new dissidents' have viewed their whiteness 'as a problem to be solved rather than as a thing to be explained' (2010: 13). Citing Martínez's article as the origin of this tendency in critical discussions of the alter-globalization movement, Thompson argues that 'indictments of the movement premised on its whiteness' have led too often to obvious, moralizing, and abstract calls to 'make organizing efforts more inclusive' (2010: 13–14). While inclusivity is surely not unimportant and the disproportionate whiteness of the movement in the global North not in question, the 'rush to inclusion', Thompson argues, has obscured the 'specificity of the problem itself', namely 'why it was that so many white kids got caught up in the struggle in the first place' (2010: 13–14). In his work, Thompson takes up this question, affirming that while the alter-globalization movement was clearly more than one-dimensional, its role as a 'laboratory' in which white middle-class activists sought to 'exorcize their constitutive contradictions and regain the capacity for political being' cannot be responsibly ignored (2010: 15). Indeed, Thompson insightfully contends that denunciations of the movement's whiteness and calls for greater inclusion and diversity actually reaffirm whiteness's invisibility, privilege and universality by denying its specificity 'in favor of what are perceived to be the greater, more grounded, and real specificities of the included other' (2010: 15). What results is not simply a delegitimation of activism emerging from relatively privileged social actors but a failure to understand how, why and with what consequences those actors might seek to enact and advance a radical, liberatory politics.

Rather than defending the abstract category of the white radical, Thompson seeks to dwell in the specificity of the experience of such dissidents in order to explore critically the routes some activists travel in pursuit of genuine politics. In so doing, he also offers important critiques of vague concepts like 'the local' and 'community', which he argues have been fetishized and made to stand in for 'the real site of struggle', always outside of the spaces and places occupied by the white middle class itself (2010: 81–2). Since 'the local' is not seen as an element of white middle-class experience, activists often sought it elsewhere, thus abandoning their own social location and experiences and relevant sources for projects of dissent, disruption and change; furthermore, since 'the local' required content, it was often envisioned in the form of engagement with 'oppressed communities', often without any recognition that the very concept of 'the community' homogenized difference and occluded power relations within the community in question, erasing the very specificity and groundedness that white middle-class activists sought to experience (2010: 81–2). In Thompson's words: 'For many activists, "the local" became an attribute of the Other and "the community" became a source of truth' (2010: 82). Through 'ideological thinking', Thompson asserts, abstract categories are substituted for complex social realities, resulting in the fetishization and valorization of the imagined oppressed Other, which stands in for the subject and social location of authentic social justice struggle (2010: 85). The consequence of this move is more than theoretically significant. Thompson notes that in homogenizing and romanticizing communities facing the cutting edge of structural violence, activists have actually worked to obscure forms of oppression that take place within them (2010: 99). This kind of ideological thinking could even be said to entrench and perpetuate systems of oppression. Thompson also takes aim at attempts to take on constituted power via identity politics, advancing the critique that because a politics rooted in identity lionizes specific subject positions located antagonistically in relation to the dominant order, marginality and victimization become defining elements which ironically and tragically allows them to be internalized into the system's very logic (2010: 120).

A number of observations might be made here regarding the 'temporality' of movement reproduction. These examples illustrate, to our mind, the fundamental tension we outlined in Chapter 3: that movements are both an intervention in the reproduction of social life and an alternative space (or, better, an alternative 'time') of social reproduction in and of themselves. The example of white activism addressed by Thompson is animated by a certain blindness to this tension. Here the normative white middle class becomes the unquestionable 'centre' of time, from which the (romanticized) reproduction of the peripheral 'local communities' (of Others) can be assayed. Yet this positioning itself helps to reproduce the white middle-class privilege and undermine the solidarity its bearers claim to yearn for. Here, anti-racist concern and rhetoric, allegedly wielded to transform social reproduction on the whole, is mobilized to furnish middle-class white youth with the means to reproduce themselves in novel but ineffective ways, to establish anti-racist identities and frames of thought that are, ultimately, of limited use in transforming social reproduction more broadly. Too often failing to take the time to build substantive relational solidarity, they limit their efficacy and radical potential.

In his scathing critique of racism awareness training (RAT), Ambalavaner Sivanandan (1990) illuminates the flawed presumptions and the dangerous consequences of an uncritical subscription to supposedly anti-oppressive practice and analysis that actually serve as a Trojan Horse for liberalism. Writing prior to the emergence of the cycle of radicalism associated with the alter-globalization movement, Sivanandan locates the rise of a certain type of anti-oppressive practice as a consequence of the 'class war going on within Marxism' over 'who – in the period of the deconstruction of industrial capitalism and the recomposition of the working class – are the real agents of revolutionary change', the no-longer-orthodox working class or the new social forces embodied by new social movements (1990: 77). In a critique that actually prefigures those that would emerge more than a decade later provoked by Michael Hardt and Antonio Negri's (2000) theorization of Empire and the multitude, Sivanandan asserts that this 'class war' was provoked both by the collapse of actually existing state socialism and the 'receding prospect of capturing state power in late capitalist societies where such power was becoming increasingly diffuse and opaque' (1990: 77). The result of this conflicted search for the new subject of revolution, argues Sivanandan, led to 'a variant of social democracy under the rubric of Eurocommunism', accompanied by a theoretical rereading of Marx, a rehashing of Gramsci, 'and a return to intellectual rigour accompanied by activist mortis'

(1990: 77). Sivanandan's withering description of what he sees as the end result of this move bears quoting at length:

> The working class, as a consequence, was stripped of its richest political seams – black, feminist, gay, green etc. – and left, in the name of anti-economism, a prey to economism. Conversely, the new social forces, freed from the ballast of economic determinism (and class reductionism), have been floated as the political and ideological 'classes' of the new radicalism. But the flight from class has served only to turn ideological priorities into idealistic preoccupations, and political autonomy into personalised politics and palliatives – which, for all that, have passed into common Left currency.... The clearest expression of these tendencies and the mortality they bring to the new social movements is to be seen in the philosophy and practice of Racism Awareness Training (RAT), the blight of the black struggle – itself a result of the flight of race from class. (1990: 77–8)

Writing in the context of the UK but with an analysis that speaks to trends much more broadly, Sivanandan argues that liberal initiatives – from multiculturalism to anti-discrimination action to other equal-opportunity programs – only play around the 'cultural fringes of discrimination – so that you could wear a turban and still get a job' (1990: 85).

Critical to Sivanandan's analysis is his excavation of the origins of RAT, locating its origins not in grassroots struggles for social justice but in the Human Awareness Training (HAT) programme that began on US military bases at the end of the 1960s in response to fears that the 'black rebellion' that was sweeping US cities would reverberate within military structures as well (1990: 98). While celebrating the trappings of diversity and difference, this institutionalized approach to racism refused to engage them as elements in a system of oppression and exploitation. Instead, racism was defined as a 'white problem' but operationalized as a personalized mental health issue or personality defect, not a structural issue of power and privilege. The critical role played by forms of oppression in building and maintaining exploitative systems was nowhere in sight for the liberal capitalist state and its beneficiaries. As Sivanandan rhetorically poses, 'what better way could the state find to smooth out its social discordances while it carried on, untrammelled, with its capitalist works?' (1990: 104). Branding RAT and its familial liberal, state-based treatments of racism-as-illness 'psychospiritual mumbo-jumbo' that mistakes personal gratification for social liberation, Sivanandan lays bare in starkly critical terms the nature of the problem at hand:

> racism is not ... a white problem, but a problem of an exploitative white power structure; power is not something white people are born into, but that which they derive from their position in a complex race/sex/class hierarchy; oppression does not equal exploitation; ideas do not equal ideology; the personal is not the political, but the political is personal; and personal liberation is not political liberation. (1990: 114)

Sivanandan draws a crucial distinction between two key and often confused terms: *racialism* is the 'prejudiced attitudes' individuals display, which in themselves have no intrinsic power; *racism* refers to 'structures and institutions with the power to discriminate', including laws, constitutional conventions, judicial precedents and institutional practices (1990: 114). This distinction is critical not only in terms of peeling interpersonal attitudes and actions away from the structural and institutional context that makes them possible, but also with respect to understanding what racism is and how it relates to the subjects it affects.

For statist and liberalist approaches like RAT or the variations of anti-oppressive praxis derived from it, racism is often cast as 'a combination of mental illness, original sin and biological determinism' with roots in a timeless, eternal 'white culture', thus rendering racism 'part of the collective unconscious, the pre-natal scream, original sin' of whites (1990: 116–17). That being so, whites can never escape racism or be anything more than 'anti-racist racists' while racism itself becomes coded at best as a cultural pathology, and at worst as an individual failure to reform oneself (1990: 116–17). Absent from such an approach is a consideration of the actual systems, institutions, structures and interests that breed and perpetuate racism. It is from this structural and institutional framework, ultimately upheld by the state, that oppressors in a racist society derive their power; yet in a capitalist state the analysis needs to be taken a step further to recognize that oppression is intimately related to the exploitative structure itself, and thus that 'racial oppression cannot be disassociated from class exploitation' (1990: 114). Interventions aimed at changing people's attitudes about others ultimately have little impact on the larger racist structure because they don't begin to touch the power relations at the heart of the oppressive–exploitative system. Of course, there remain possibilities for oppressors in RAT and other liberal approaches to racialism: catharsis, a catalyst for personal change regarding the treatment of others, perhaps even a route to political activism for those already so inclined. But any claim to do more than this, argues Sivanandan, is nothing more than a 'delusion of grandeur' and a 'betrayal of political black struggle against racism' (1990: 115). Making the distinction between racialism and racism – between interpersonal attitudes and behaviours and power relations between classes – is critical strategically and tactically in terms of setting priorities in struggle, and also clarifying the nature of the struggle itself so that the state and the capitalist interests it serves do not play one strand against the other (1990: 115).

The making of time

From these arguments we may make an initial distinction between the practices of 'making space' for diversity and 'making time' for anti-oppression. The idea or ideal of 'making space' is reflective of the drive to 'open up' movements to a greater plurality of participants, presumably to better mirror the reigning demographics, or even to highlight the importance of confronting patriarchy, racism, colonialism or other forms of structural oppression within society. 'Making space' implies that a movement thinks reflexively and self-critically about the way its organizational structure, group dynamics, forms of engagement and priorities might be barriers to diverse communities and individuals.

Yet the idea of 'making space' shares with notions like 'tolerance', 'multiculturalism' and 'inclusion' an inherent normative assumption: organizations and movements are properly grounded and oriented; they simply need to 'open up' and become 'more accepting' of difference or, at best, 'add' various forms of oppression (transphobia, ablism, colonialism) to their core analysis (Bannerji 2000; Philip 1992). 'Making space' implies that there is already a space that needs expanding, a house that simply requires an extra room to be added on to the back to make space for a new guest or an adopted family member. What is generally missing from such approaches is a sense that addressing oppression requires a much more fundamental, 'ground-up' rebuilding of analysis, organization, strategy and orientation. Movements all too often fall prey to the liberal narrative and progressivist temporality which suggests that 'once we were exclusive, but now we are inclusive'. This creates a false break between an imagined past when prejudice, ignorance and exclusivity prevented oppressed people from coming into the space, and a blissful present when 'we' are perfectly inclusive, merely awaiting the arrival of our overdue brothers and sisters.

This orientation conveniently makes the lack of participation by oppressed people the fault and responsibility of oppressed people themselves. If space is made, the failure to fill it becomes the failure of oppressed people to overcome *their* prejudices and recalcitrance and recognize their own best interests are served through participation. Hence, we need to reimagine anti-oppression less as a matter of making space and more as a matter of making *time*. The irony, of course, is that time cannot be 'made'; yet the metaphor of 'finding time' doesn't do justice to the degree of agency and intentionality required. Rather, the work of anti-oppression, if it is to be effective, must take up time, must preoccupy movements that might believe they have 'more important' work to attend to. It is precisely in the capacity of anti-oppression to impose, to delay and to make us impatient that its transformative power lies. Making time for anti-oppression would mean an inherent understanding that this time is, in actuality, endless. As anti-oppression authors and educators remind us, the idea of ever fully overcoming sexism, racism, ableism or other vectors of oppression is a myth: we are born and bred of an oppressive culture which necessarily conscripts us on multiple levels in order to carry out its reproduction. Work dedicated to anti-oppression is an endless project. So making time for it does not simply act as some sort of penance for original and eternal sin, providing absolution. Rather, comprehending the endless nature of oppression reorients our imagination regarding what solidarity might mean. In other words, anti-oppressive politics, if they are to be meaningful, must be part and parcel of a transformation of temporality, our sense of who and what is worthy of our time, a shift in what we imagine to be critical to struggle and what we imagine to be a distraction.

The incubation of oppressions within movement spaces – the failure to make time to confront them and the systems of power they reproduce – is a powerful barrier to the realization of solidarity between diverse individuals and collectives who, otherwise, would seem to share common cause. In his path-breaking work on the phenomenon, David Featherstone (2012) describes 'solidarity' not as a thing to be achieved but as 'a relation forged through political struggle which seeks to challenge forms of oppression' (2012: 5) – in other words, solidarity not as a space but as a temporality. Drawing on a wealth of historical and contemporary examples of struggles for social justice located primarily, though not exclusively, in the north Atlantic world, Featherstone contends that solidarity is a transformative relationship which may be about a recognition of 'likeness' among the actors involved but which is also about 'constructing relations between' disparate 'places, activists, diverse social groups' (2012: 5). Importantly, while solidarity has the capacity to transform relations between actors and 'the active creation of new ways of relating,' it can also cement 'existing identities and power relations' (2012: 5). Solidarity is thus no guaranteed path to liberation, even within movement spaces where it is successfully realized. This does not mean it is not powerful or that it is not capable of challenging and transforming structures of oppression and exploitation outside of and within social movements, but given that it is a relationship articulated across difference − difference that frequently also implies uneven power relations − its practice does not signify the upending of all injustices. In this sense, it is possible and eminently realistic to forge solidaristic relations among diverse individuals and collectives engaged in struggle without expecting such relations to be free from contradiction. Put another way, the endurance of oppressive relations in the context of a struggle linked through the articulation of solidarity does not signal the failure of those struggles or a failure of solidarity. In spite of power relations, oppression and exploitation, Featherstone's exploration demonstrates just how 'inventive' the construction of solidarity can be, producing 'new ways of configuring political relations and spaces' and reshaping 'the terrain of what is politically possible and what counts or is recognized as political' (2012: 7). The perpetuation of unjust relations and structures within social movement spaces and times, as well as within society at large, remains a primary site in the struggle for social justice and liberation. However, it would be a mistake to conflate the persistence of such relations and systems with a complete failure of radical politics.

Here we might reflect on the way that social movements inherently create different spaces of temporality or 'chronotopes', to borrow a term coined by Mikhail Bakhtin (1981). Chrono-topes represent social spheres animated by a shared imagination of time. An idea initially developed to describe the particular landscape of temporality germane to literary genres, this term can be expanded to speak to the way we share a conception and feeling of the flow of events and the passage of time. In other words, a chronotope represents an unspoken agreement or ambient shared sense of how history moves, how individuals and groups develop and change, how the past informs the present and shapes the future, and what might ultimately be possible. While social movements all too often reproduce the forms of exclusion, oppression and exploitation, and inequality germane to the society they seek to change, their commitment to challenge social norms and power structures renders them spaces where alternative temporalities might be imagined. Further, Featherstone's analysis reveals that this new temporality, if it is to produce solidarity, has no end point. Solidarity is not the achievement of an anti-oppressive space; it is the ceaseless dedication to confronting oppression that, so long as we live in a society that reproduces itself through oppression and privilege, will necessarily continue to haunt and vex the reproduction of social movements.

In conversation with activist and historian Staughton Lynd, academic and activist Andrej Grubačić offers a conceptualization of 'humanitarian activism' that further illuminates the importance of solidarity as a potentially transformative relationship. 'Humanitarian activism', Grubačić contends, 'promotes an internationalism of guilt' rather than seeking to transform the power relations at the root of systems of oppression and exploitation. He continues:

It is a peculiar intellectual and political habit of identifying a 'noble revolutionary savage,' both at home and someplace else – and the word 'community' seems to always signify 'someplace else' – while abandoning common people at home, in search of a more exotic functional equivalent.... There seems to exist an unfortunate peculiarity of the American activist simultaneously to support guerrilla movements abroad and behave like a social worker, tending the communities from the outside, not as a fellow student or fellow worker with a particular understanding of a situation shared with others, but as a professional organizer, a force outside of society, organizing those 'inside' on their own behalf. (Lynd and Grubačić 2008: 163)

In this passage, Grubačić, like Thompson, incisively critiques tendencies within a contemporary activist culture that still yearns for a 'real' revolutionary subject who always seems to exist 'somewhere else' in something akin to an authentic revolutionary state of nature. From the perspective of what Grubačić labels 'humanitarian activism', those with relative privilege cannot be really revolutionary themselves; instead, they must find someone and somewhere else to invest with all the hopes and dreams of the revolutionary struggle they desire but which they cannot see in the contradiction and complexity of their own lives, and then seek to assist, organize and facilitate the struggle from without. At issue here is a central tension. On the one hand, it has been tempting for movements to declare the time for anti-oppression 'over', offering conclusive strategies or seeking to defer anti-oppressive work until 'after' some allegedly more important change. On the other hand, there is an equally pernicious tendency to render anti-oppression an endless chore, a constant, disciplinary 'work of the self' with almost evangelical overtones of sin, guilt, penance and (ever-deferred) redemption. These two tendencies, which at first may seem diametrically opposed, are a mutually supporting pillars of a broader chronotope that actually militates against the building of substantive solidarities that might have the power to present a real challenge to oppression and exploitation in society at large. As Grubačić illustrates, these temptations are bound up in a romantic and fetishistic understanding of power and oppression that all too often gravitates towards the search for the single key form of oppression, exploitation or abjection, which can unlock the riddle of effective radical action.

For his part, Staughton Lynd, drawing on his own rich experience as a veteran social justice activist, offers an approach to building solidarity across difference that he names 'accompaniment'. For Lynd, accompaniment 'is simply the idea of walking side by side with another on a common journey'. It presumes not 'uncritical deference' to one actor or another 'but equality', with the expectation that differences in experience, formal and informal education, skills and more will allow each participant to contribute significantly to the struggle (Lynd and Grubačić 2008: 176–7). For Lynd, then, there is no privileged epistemic location, no site to prioritize in anchoring the struggle, except in the sense that real rather than rhetorical struggles for social justice are always located geographically, socially and politically and lie at the intersection of multiple and overlapping systems of oppression and exploitation. As for confronting and overcoming entrenched systems of oppression as they reproduce themselves within the fabric of social movements and social justice struggles, Lynd contends that 'people can overcome differences in race, ethnicity, religion, and for that matter, anything else, on the basis of shared experience.

Usually it is a common experience of oppression that brings people together.... The question, of course, is: When [people] come back to ordinary civilian life ... what then?' (2008: 179). If solidarity can be forged in the context of struggle with difference no longer functioning as an axis of oppression, how can this experience be used to frame new ways of relating to one another outside of the specificity of a given struggle for social justice? In our terms, how can the time of solidarity be extended to encompass the time of ordinary life?

Lynd's notion of 'accompaniment' and 'walking side by side with another on a common journey' echo the Zapatista principles of *preguntando caminamos* ('asking, we walk') and *caminar al paso del mas lento* ('walking at the pace of the slowest'). Radical social transformation, a transformation that *matters* and that changes the way society as a whole is reproduced, is ultimately an endless journey filled with questions, but one that is animated by the task of building solidarity and relationality. In other words, rather than seeking to build perfect political rhetoric and organization, rather than designing iron-clad movement architectures which might include the seductive ornamentation of anti-oppressive rhetoric, the task is to take time. Overcoming the crisis of social reproduction in society at large, and the reproduction of oppression that is so central to it, is neither about developing a flawless strategy to be enacted from on high nor about making one's movements into a cozy zone of reproduction allegedly free of all oppression. Rather, struggle (as we discussed in Chapter 4) is about failing, and failing better, to build solidarity, to embrace a temporality of perseverance and militancy that recognizes and makes time for contradiction.

The hazard, of course, is falling prey to what Mark Fisher (2013) calls the 'Vampire Castle': a metaphor for the self-cannibalizing subculture of anti-oppression that has, in his reading, preoccupied the left since the 'anarchist turn' we noted above. For Fisher, anti-oppression, far from its roots in class struggle, has all too often become a means for movements and individuals to create pathological, obsessive and judgemental cliques that worry themselves to death (or into undeath) by expecting an impossible perfection from all involved. While Fisher is no doubt correct in many ways, we are not willing to relinquish the important work anti-oppressive frameworks can and do perform within movements. Such frameworks, when they are dedicated to transforming and empowering collectives (rather than setting up new hierarchies of knowledge and prestige), do not simply 'correct' mistakes or 'failures' within organizations or individuals; they fundamentally transform the shared temporality of movements.

Reproducing otherwise:
beyond oppression and exploitation

For long-time social justice and anti-oppression activist and educator Anne Bishop (2002), oppression within social movements as well as in the context of society at large is the 'inevitable result of "power-over"', domination or force exercised either by oppressors or by those in resistance (2002: 42). Bishop distinguishes between 'power-over' and three other key types of power: 'power-within,' one's 'centredness' and 'grounding in one's own beliefs, wisdom, knowledge, skills, culture, and community'; 'power-with', which is 'exercised cooperatively among equals'; and 'authority', which is 'the wisdom, creativity, or expression of a group's energy by an individual that is recognized and agreed to by others as right at a certain time' (2002: 42). Bishop argues that in order to end oppression we need to collectively 'discover how we can restore the skills, methods, and culture of "power-with"' (2002: 44). Critically, Bishop engages oppression – manifested via political power, economic power, physical force and ideological power – not as the outcome of interpersonal dynamics or a failure of 'tolerance' but as a 'world of systems' whose sole purpose is to preserve structured injustice and inequality designed to benefit the few at the expense of the great many (2002: 51).

Within many social justice movement spaces, the politics and practice of anti-oppression have often run up against those who contend that prioritizing the struggle against diverse and seemingly proliferating oppressions occludes the importance of the struggle against systematic forms of injustice and exploitation. In more basic terms, those who see class and capitalism as the proper targets of struggle have cast anti-oppression politics and practice as self-help therapy that mystifies and misidentifies the real sources of oppression and exploitation. Broadly speaking, this division has often been cast as those working from a more Marxist, class-based politics and those whose activism and analysis orbit around a less economically deterministic, more identity-based conception of social justice and social change. While this crude distinction homogenizes what are much more complex and nuanced positions, it serves the purpose of illuminating a tension around the question of temporality in contemporary radical social justice activism.

For our purposes, this division demonstrates the utter necessity of the Marxist-feminist notion of 'reproduction'. As long as we continue to fetishize the 'working class' as the 'producers' of social value and centre our analysis of capital around the exploitation of waged labour, we will continue to exalt a historically anachronistic and presently reductionist (generally white, male) 'subject of history' as the ultimate bearer of revolutionary potential. From the perspective of Mies, Federici and others, we would more properly interpret the labour of the industrial working class as a product of a globalized division of reproductive labour. While capitalism may be based on the commodification of time and of objects, the manufacture of goods by waged workers is a misrecognized act of social reproduction: when we make something together, whether in a factory or a kitchen or in a field or in a theatre, we are reproducing our social world. While the specificities and struggles of each zone of reproduction must be addressed individually, and while the struggles of the industrial manufacturers is central to the project of liberation, capitalism works, fundamentally, by creating artificial, alienating and unequal divisions between *all those who labour.* In this sense, we can broaden our conception of the 'working class' to include all those who reproduce social life, though not under conditions of their own choosing. We can recognize that it is the mission of the working class to liberate its labour from the thrall of capital without reducing that working class merely to those who produce actual commodities, and indeed such a perspective allows us to better understand the expansion of capitalist commodification into the realms of social reproduction through the expansion of the (feminized, racialized) service sector and the commercialization of the domestic sphere and society at large.

Within this framework, we can also see the reproduction of oppression as critical to the reproduction of the capitalist system more broadly. Racism, sexism, homophobia and other forms of oppression do not simply separate 'workers' from one another; nor do they simply cheapen the labour of some to facilitate its ready exploitation by others. The reproduction of oppression is the very nature of exploitation: the creation of false differences, differential patterns of privation and privilege, and the fostering of oppressive and oppressed subjects are the means by which capital reproduces itself. Hence the distinction between 'oppression' and 'exploitation' is never simple or transparent. The two articulate one another as the system seeks to reproduce itself amidst continual crises, both those caused by its own internal, inherent contradictions, and those caused by the constancy of resistance and solidarity.

Significantly, Bishop's own analysis focuses not on a false dichotomy between oppression and exploitation but on their mutually constitutive nature. As she explains:

> on a structural level, class is different from other forms of oppression such as racism, ageism, and sexism. Class is not just a factor in inequalities in wealth, privilege, and power; it *is* that inequality. Other forms of oppression help keep the hierarchy of power in place; class is that hierarchy. Class is the beginning point and end product of all other forms of oppression. It is the essential structure of society, the sum total of all the other inequalities.... The other oppressions are building tools; class is the wall. The other oppressions are cause and effect; class is the resulting structure. The other oppressions make it possible for some people to justify having access to the resources of others; class is the fact that they have that access. We must deal with

the cultural aspects of class, but class is not just another form of oppression. (2002: 82–4)

Rather than focusing on any specific oppression and working from it as the site for the elaboration of a new liberatory politics, Bishop foregrounds injustice, exploitation and inequality as the core of the system of 'power-over' designed to serve the interests of the few at the expense of the many, a system supported by an elaborate structure of mutually constitutive oppressions whose key role is to legitimize the exploitation and violence directed at the dispossessed. Oppression is thus not something that some people do because they don't know any better; rather, oppression is actualized in order to reproduce the operation of the dominant system. Oppression is not an identity that one adopts and can simply unlearn or abandon through better behaviour; it is the outcome of structural power relations. While members of an oppressor group (for example, men in a patriarchal society; whites in a racist society) can be allies of those oppressed, they remain oppressors so long as the system that accords them their privilege remains in place. At the same time, every oppressor can also be oppressed (for example, someone may be privileged as a man and oppressed as a result of his sexual preference) and every member of the oppressed can also be an oppressor (for example, someone who is oppressed as a consequence of her racialized identity but who exercises power-over as a result of her economic power).

Thus, Bishop is not talking about identity as the key axis of oppression; rather, she illuminates oppression as the expression of a system designed to preserve and entrench power over others. In her work, Bishop itemizes the qualities that make for good allies in the struggle against oppression as well as the characteristics that make for productive and powerful alliances for the oppressed when working with would-be allies. With regard to would-be allies, in addition to counselling avoidance of the tendency to deny oppression and privilege or to wallow in guilt, Bishop foregrounds the importance of social structures, histories and collective responsibility. She stresses the necessity of collective action based on the acknowledgement and unpacking of privilege and the need to be wary of the power of allies to inadvertently take ownership of or romanticize liberation struggles (2002: 114–19). For the oppressed in the context of working with allies, Bishop urges clarity with respect to deciding 'if, why, when, and how' to work with allies and learning to discern who is really an ally and who constitutes the enemy. This would necessarily be based in acting with a strong knowledge of self, in a spirit of kindness, and refusing the tendency to homogenize members of an oppressor group (2002: 119–20). Bishop's steps for allies and the oppressed in the struggle against systems of power-over revolve around critically understanding one's own social location as a product of structured power relations that by their very nature implicate others across time and space in a complex calculus of privilege and exploitation.

For movements, Bishop emphasizes the importance of hope, not merely in an abstract sense but in terms of balancing the important 'intellectual work' of analysis, strategy and critique necessary to social justice struggle with the 'openness and fun' critical to sustaining movements as social collectives which require 'affirmation, acceptance, tolerance, pleasure, joy, humour, release, creativity, and fun' (2002: 148–9). The kind of balance that Bishop articulates here is intimately wrapped up with issues of time and space within social movements. It is not enough simply to celebrate the significance of hope, camaraderie, laughter and love. Movement participants have to devote time, resources and energy in order to envision and then build the structures and processes adequate to realizing the balance.

To conclude, one more point might be raised regarding the times of oppression and exploitation. Within the traditional Marxist framework, time is the central axis of exploitation: the system reproduces itself by reducing the cooperative labour of social reproduction to the universalized, abstracted and alienated substance of abstract labour power. The individuality of and the difference between workers is reduced to its most basic rudiments (such as on an assembly line, where tasks are 'deskilled' and broken into tiny parts). Abstract labour power is, at least theoretically, measured by 'socially necessary labour time', which is in turn the source of value under capitalism. The capitalist takes the value produced by abstract(ed) labour and sells it, pocketing the surplus value and giving the worker barely enough to reproduce him- or herself and, perhaps, their family. The surplus is then reinvested by the capitalist in the reproduction of capital: either s/he spends it on expanding the enterprise or invests it, allowing a bank or financial firm to lend it out to another capitalist for similar purposes.

We have already outlined the substantial limits to such a perspective, but two key observations emerge here. The first is that time remains the key axis of capitalist exploitation. It is the system's ability to make us trade our time (in terms of time working for someone else or otherwise making money) that gives it such power over social reproduction. This inculcates the pervasive sense that time is a scarce 'resource' to be hoarded and never wasted, a perception that haunts social movements as well. In a world where all our time is priced, movements fear 'investing' time in the seemingly eternal struggle against oppression. But such a fear is symptomatic. As Harsha Walia notes (2013: 173–202), the myths of scarcity are central to the breakdown of social movements, and it is vital to cultivate an ethos of abundance in order to do the work of solidarity. It is no doubt true that movements cannot and should not dedicate all their time to self-flagellation over real or perceived failures to make time for anti-oppression. But what we are arguing here is that the struggle against oppression requires we reimagine time and temporality (as well as the very meaning of failure) if we are to effectively grow strong anti-oppressive movements. So long as we inherit and fail to question the temporality of capitalism and its mythology of scarcity and sacrifice, we will continue to reproduce movements that sacrifice anti-oppression to the idol of political necessity.

The second observation is this: at the heart of capitalist exploitation is a logic of indifference. Capitalism generates value by erasing differences and reducing each of us to our capacity to contribute time to the (re)production of capital. While capitalism explicitly mobilizes difference to secure exploitation (emblematized by the figures of the sweatshop garment worker, the 'temporary' migrant agricultural worker, and the 'guest' domestic care worker, to name only a few) at its core, it works by transforming human time into a universal and indifferent commodity. As such, the struggle against economic exploitation is also necessarily a struggle *for* difference, and not merely in the liberal idiom of a boutique, commodified and superficial celebration of 'difference' that is always already reconciled within the confines of the established order (Fish 1997). The struggle against exploitation is therefore always also a struggle against oppression. They meet each other at a shared horizon where we envision a world where individuals and communities are free to cooperate and define themselves on their own terms, rather than having structure and meaning imposed upon them from afar. This horizon is the pluralization and abundance of difference.

Ultimately, oppression and exploitation are tools used to capture our cooperative and reproductive capacities in the service of some overarching and self-perpetuating system over which we have little control and whose benefits are profoundly unequally distributed. The antidote to both exploitation and oppression is the combination of solidarity and autonomy: cooperating otherwise, reproducing our social and individual lives on our own shared terms. The constant process of (re)discovering how to build grassroots autonomy and solidarity is well worth the time.

PART FOUR

The methods of movements

SEVEN

Imagination, strategy and tactics

Many methods aimed at studying social movements treat them like objects in a shadow box: as fixed, static and self-contained entities that can be dissected to reveal their inner workings, even if those inner workings are themselves obscure or unacknowledged by movement participants themselves (see Chapter 1). In Chapter 2, we outlined how our approach differs not only from the more positivist and quantitative methods, but also from many qualitative and ethnographic methods. We then advanced a strategy for 'convoking' the radical imagination *with* social movements by building a reflexive and responsive relationship between the researcher and the movement(s) in question.

Both a strength and a weakness of the more conservative social scientific approaches to research is their rigorous attention to methodological thinking – that is, the explicit attention they pay to questions of how we know what we claim to know, what counts as reliable evidence, and how we can most effectively interpret phenomena. While these questions are rarely framed in explicitly critical (let alone radical) ways, the empirical demands they make can be important correctives to ideological thinking. Methodological thinking is a weakness because it often leads to mechanical patterns and approaches to exploring social realities, approaches that are often bound up with the hubris of the researcher who, imagining him- or herself as situated outside of history and society, uses sophisticated tools to 'look in'. The strength of a focus on method lies in a more thorough and systematic way of putting the pieces of the world together, and, taken in moderation, this can be a good thing. What intentional methodological thinking ideally provides is a rigorous and constructively sceptical perspective on what we think we know and how we came to know it. This is not positivism – the facile and dangerous belief in a singular truth that we can find with the right tool; it is the best legacy of empiricism, the conviction that we can know about the world we inhabit through our intentional explorations of it, and that we can hone the ways in which we carry out these explorations. In what follows, we attempt to show how some of the basic methodological principles of the social sciences can be used by both social movement researchers and social movements themselves to reimagine solidarity.

We suggest that, in the same way that the methodological imagination is shaped by questions of the relationship between ontology, epistemology and methodology, so too can social movement thinkers (both researchers and participants) reimagine the links between the imagination, strategies and tactics and the tensions between them. We want here to move towards a cobbled-together, imperfect prototype of what might be called a 'prefigurative methodology', a methodology borrowed from the future we should like to see created, brought back into the present to help make that future a possibility. Such a methodology would be one that, ironically, imagines a society which would have radically transformed the university and the idea of 'research' itself, dispersing teaching, learning, critical debate, and systematic, rigorous inquiry throughout the fabric of social reproduction, rather than in the elitist ivory tower. If, as we have argued, radical social movements today foster and enliven the radical imagination by striving to be spaces of alternative social reproduction, how can social movement research be part of this process and help reproduce a difference world?

From ontology to epistemology to methods to ethics

Research inherently begins with a notion of 'ontology'. Ontology is a philosophy of 'being', one's conception of reality. A religious fundamentalist, for instance, might imagine that the world is driven by God's will, or by a conflict between God and the Devil, and that we are all merely actors in a melodrama of good and evil. By contrast, Marxian-inspired and feminist scholars might argue that social reality is really based around the division of labour (who does what sort of work and how is that work organized?) and the distribution of the fruits of that labour (who is rich, who is poor, etc.). More liberal scholars might imagine, in the tradition of sociologists like Max Weber, that social life is made up of symbolic interactions – that is, by individuals making meaning out of their relationships with one another and the structures of social life that they build. Ontology represents how one imagines the driving forces of society, the agents and causes of change, and the expected outcomes of social actions.

One's ontological approach will, in turn, help determine one's 'epistemology'. Epistemology is a philosophy of knowledge. How can we know something to be true? How can we describe and define social reality? What sorts of texts, methods and experiences provide us with reliable information? And what sorts of evidence count? For instance, to revisit our religious fundamentalist, his ontological assumption that the social world is a contest between divine and diabolical forces justifies the epistemological understanding of a religious text as the literal word of God, making this document into an unassailable, unquestionable source of truth. Likewise, he may also believe that even seemingly highly reliable scientific knowledge (such as the carbon dating of dinosaur bones whose age appears to contradict the Bible's chronology of creation) is not only untrustworthy but even devilishly and maliciously false. Likewise, if one was of the ontological belief that human behaviour and social interaction are primarily expressions of our DNA (as do many sociobiologists and evolutionary psychologists) and that humans are essentially vehicles for the reproduction of genes through procreation, then one's epistemological approach would imagine the nuances of art, culture, the humanities, and other forms of human creative and cultural activity as largely irrelevant. From this perspective, the ontological 'truth' of us as a species resides in our genetic code, with science's job to map and interpret this data. As we can see, one's ontological assumptions shape one's epistemological approach. What one thinks exists in the social world will inform what sorts of information and data one thinks are valuable, reliable, admissible and useful.

Already one can see there is room for disagreement. For instance, many sociologists – in the Weberian tradition – agree ontologically that social reality is made up of individuals' relationships to social institutions. But some might believe that the only way to discover this is through large quantitative data sets, because the experience and dynamics of social institutions are inherently beyond the understanding of any one individual. Others believe that the testimony and narratives of individuals are a better guide, noting that the complexities of the biographies of individuals are the best means to understanding the nuances of institutional structures. This is not merely a difference between 'macro' and 'micro' sociological scales, it is a difference between how one understands the constitution of social reality, what can be known about it, and how.

More politically, the difference between ontologies and epistemologies has resulted in many conflicts. For instance, for the vast majority of modern history, and even to this day, Western knowledge systems make the ontological assumption that Indigenous peoples around the world have a more 'primitive' social structure and, as a result, that their traditional forms of knowledge are epistemologically unreliable. Hence oral testimony, allegorical stories, the knowledge of elders or the power of dreams are all discounted as worthless (see Lal 2002). There are, of course, profound material consequences to this. As Linda Tuhiwai Smith (2012) has eloquently noted, the discounting of Indigenous epistemologies has been absolutely central to genocide, theft of land, destruction of culture and the devaluation of Indigenous people. If oral traditions and Indigenous political and legal systems are dismissed as fundamentally unreliable, then Indigenous peoples' claims to land rights or self-determination are granted only at the whim of the settler-colonial state and its legal and governmental system.

Another example can be found in the early days of second-wave feminism. In a patriarchal intellectual environment, women's ideas and understandings of their own experience and of the world were fundamentally devalued and distrusted. When feminists began to organize, a key means to do so was to create women-only spaces for 'consciousness-raising', allowing women to discuss and affirm their shared experience of oppression, violence, devaluation and anger (Rebick 2005). These became spaces to recognize and build an alternative ontology (the idea that the social order was fundamentally based on gendered oppression, exploitation and inequality) and epistemology (that women's experience and knowledge were valid and important) (Harding 2006). So social movements, too, root themselves in the interplay between ontological and epistemological assumptions. That is, social movements can sometimes cohere around a shared experience (ontology) of injustice, or they can be sites or networks in which knowledge of shared experience can be recognized and validated (epistemology). Alexis Shotwell (2011), among others, has written cogently on the important co-resonances between situated epistemologies and struggles around race, gender and sexuality: knowing the world 'otherwise' is a reflexive element of both radical movements and radical writing.

To return to research, we teach social science students that, once they have determined their ontological and epistemological orientation, they can then build a method to fit, one that will accurately 'measure' some ontological fact and which will be acceptable within a given epistemological framework. So, to go back to the example of our researcher who believes that all human behaviour is driven by genetics, her methods will attempt to measure the impact of a certain genetic combinations on one's hair colour preference by, for instance, running aptitude tests based on colour matching on thousands of people and correlating these results with genetic screening. Likewise, our religious fundamentalist might want to devise a method for proving that Satan is at work on the earth, and to do so might cite several passages of scripture and recount a variety of examples of people committing 'evil' acts. Feminist researchers, by contrast, might seek to test their ontological assumption that women experience oppression within the home in a way that is in keeping with their epistemological commitment to value women's experience, and so conduct interviews with a demonstrative cross-section of women not only to see if their experiences are in common, but to provide a venue for women to recognize for themselves their shared conditions.

From these examples, we can begin to discern the complicated three-way relationship between ontology, epistemology and methodology. One's ontological assumptions inform one's epistemological approach, which in turn shapes one's methodological research strategy. Typically, the data one gathers through one's research methodology will affirm or add nuance to one's ontological understanding of the world because one has an epistemological belief in the reliability of the method employed. For this reason, most research ends up confirming its researcher's basic ontological predisposition, which is one reason why research often feels so very specialized and why disciplines and sub-disciplines can become so very cloistered. For instance, the researcher who believes all human behaviour is driven by genetics and the researcher who seeks to prove Satan's presence on earth are miles apart ontologically, and so also epistemologically and methodologically, and they would likely see one another's research as totally bogus. And perhaps in this, and only this, both are entirely correct.

Radicalizing the research imagination

For our purposes, we want to suggest that the triad of ontology, epistemology and methodology encapsulate in the space between them what we call the *research imagination*. As we've argued throughout the book, the imagination is not an individual possession; it is a shared landscape, which doesn't mean that all those who share in the imagination imagine everything the same way. Imaginations overlap, conflict, contradict and communicate across time and space. Understanding ontology, epistemology and methodology as triangulating the research imagination helps us understand that, in reality, even for the most scrupulous researchers, these three categories do not function in a seamless or perfectly aligned fashion. So even our genetic behaviourist can't neatly quarantine all her own ontological and epistemological assumptions, the unspoken background against which theoretical and methodological paradigms are set and so become thinkable. Nor can she design a perfect genetic measure for behaviour that allows her to escape the consequences of this.

For instance, the vast majority of genetic research into human behaviour operates on the basis of a set of assumptions that are not only incredibly conservative but that project present power relations and inequalities into the evolutionary past, in spite of a near total absence of any evidence to support such a supposition (see Lewontin 1996). These include seeking to delimit 'legitimate' expressions of gender and sexuality,

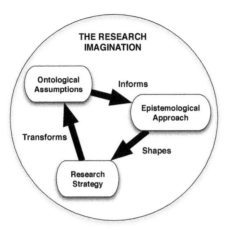

The research imagination

naturalizing patriarchy and male violence through the myth of 'man the hunter', and justifying capitalist exploitation by recourse to its imagined roots in the mists of our species' 'state of nature'. In any case, without belabouring questions germane to the 'science wars' of yesteryear, we simply want to make the case that even the most rigorous and systemic research paradigms rely, fundamentally, on something more than the sum of their parts, on a broader *imaginary* that helps order and organize thinking and that is the often invisible syntax between ontology, epistemology and methodology.

Perhaps an easier place to see this is to return to the example of feminist research. Feminist activism did not emerge *sui generis* from a miraculous ontological assumption made by a single woman one day, who then went on to develop an epistemological approach and a series of methods by which she conclusively proved the existence of patriarchy. Instead, the feminist research *imaginary* was built piece by piece by many women (and a few men, and trans folk) each contributing to its ontological assumptions, epistemological frameworks and methodological approaches. And, vitally, these activists and researchers did the important work of *multiplying* the ontological positions, epistemological orientations and methodological gambits of feminism. So anti-racist feminists insisted that the ontological experiences and epistemological orientations of non-white women were fundamentally different from those of their white counterparts (see, for example, Mohanty 2003). Queer and trans feminists likewise challenged the hetero- and cis-normative assumptions of other feminist ontologies, epistemologies and methodologies. As such, it is possible to talk about a broad, all-encompassing feminist research imagination, and also more localized research imaginations, which might overlap with other spheres, in the way anti-racist feminisms might also overlap with some dimensions of broader anti-racist struggles.

The overlaps and contradictions are of particular importance because they are the places where change can happen, where the established circuits of ontology, epistemology and methodology can be shaken up. We have argued that the imagination (especially the radical imagination) is something that we never possess but something we do (and do together). We've also argued that the radical imagination stems from the experience of difference and the struggle for solidarity. In the same way, we can think about the research imagination not so much as being defined by clear, comprehensive and cohesive alignments between ontology, epistemology and methodology, but by conflict, contention, dissensus, difference and debate.

For us, this has three important features. The first is that, while a clear delineation of ontology, epistemology and

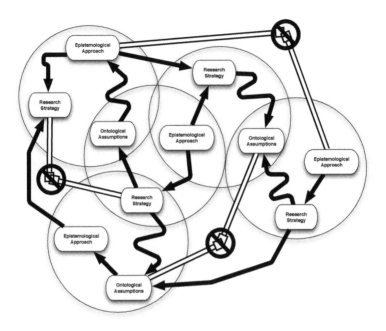

The expanded model of the research imagination

methodology is sometimes conceptually desirable, it is impossible in practice. That is, there are no perfect methods, nor should there be. The research imagination and its component parts are always being contested, strained, challenged and transformed, both from within and from without the research community. A perfect circuit of the research imagination all too often lends itself to petty (or not so petty) authoritarianism, such as the example of the religious fundamentalist or closed-minded genetic behaviourist (and, we might add, some more doctrinaire Marxists), all of whom ruthlessly excise and declare irrelevant other forms of knowledge and non-commensurable and dissonant world-views. This can have disastrous consequences, and it is no accident that these rigid methodological approaches have justified and allowed for the allegedly disinterested perpetuation and execution of great injustices. For example, as noted above, certain dominant strands of Western anthropology at once delivered up knowledge about 'native peoples' around the world and also systematically froze out their knowledge, perspectives and voices, which in turn justified a whole array of colonial acts including forced relocation, the seizure of children for re-education, the theft of land and more. The most recent incarnation of this trajectory is the practice of anthropologists going to work for Western militaries in counter-insurgency operations by 'mapping the human terrain', providing key socio-cultural and political information about populations under occupation and so constituting a vital link in the 'war on terror's' globalized chain of rendition and assassination (see Network of Concerned Anthropologists 2009; Price 2011).

Hence the 'signal' between ontology, epistemology and methodology is never pure; there is always noise, interference, static, dissonance. While the *process* of striving to achieve clarity, fidelity and alignment is extremely important, it is an impossible task. That is, while paying close, conscious attention to the work of developing a coherent and thoughtful methodology is key, the goal itself is not achievable in some final, definitive way; it is a horizon on which we fix our gaze as we walk. Keeping our ontological and epistemological orienting points firmly in view is vital to constructing a methodology that is rigorous, critical and reflexive, but we should never mistake this for the end of the journey itself. We need to be open and attentive to interruptions, failures, gaps, lacunae, sticky spots and agonism.

The second important feature of this approach is that it must necessarily inform a 'deep research ethics'. In Chapter 1 we reflected on our discomfort with and distrust of the official dimensions of much conventional academic research and its ethics, in particular the way it prioritizes 'objective' research that essentially exploits a target constituency primarily in order to generate academic capital. To this we might add our profound objection to official 'ethical' research guidelines that serve as a vehicle by which to indemnify host universities and institutions from future litigation while frequently blithely ignoring what we consider to be glaring ethical problems, such as cooperating with law enforcement agencies, doing research that benefits corporate interests, and privatizing and commodifying what ought to be common knowledge. Moreover, we also question the ethics of highly systematic and formulaic research methods which seek to transform the complexities of lived experience into esoteric models or neat datasets (or, for that matter, sexy, obscurantist theoretical jargon), but which all too often (to borrow language from the humanities) 'do violence to the text' of social relations by reducing lived experience to some mechanical husk. These methods and 'ethics' are geared towards making research work for certain interests, to render research functional, either as grist for the academic mill or for more or less odious social interests. We also believe that research should work for communities, and this demands a very different research imagination. What we might call the mainstream research imagination tries to carefully align ontology, epistemology and methodology to create highly 'reliable' specialized knowledge. In so doing, it effectively seeks to create a knowledge commodity, a discrete unit of data to enter into

a marketplace of knowledge exchange (and, like all economies, this one is far from egalitarian). The emphasis placed on
market-ready research outcomes (deliverables) by universities
and funding agencies only highlights this trend, one that is
accelerating as austerity eats into publicly funded institutions
and research and the academic marketplace becomes ever more
competitive, with each institution seeking to find a niche for its
product and secure its market share by more effectively training
the next generation of precarious, flexible workers. Instead of
this bankrupt and complicit vision of research, we advocate a
messy, conflicted, confused and contradictory research imagination, one where ontology, epistemology and methodology all
exist in dynamic tension. The product of this research is not
distinct units of knowledge but *an intervention into the flows of
the imagination itself.* That is, it sees its ethical role as both the
product of and an intervention at the intersection of multiple
imaginaries and imaginations. It seeks to be a catalyst for new
solidarities and ideas. In other words, it is built from and seeks
to stimulate the radical imagination. There is no guarantee, of
course, that this research won't be commodified, captured or
appropriated by the powers-that-be. This risk does not free us
from the responsibility to try.

The third feature of this approach is that the questions surrounding the research imagination can also be borrowed and
retooled for use in everyday life and the struggles the research
seeks to understand and reflect on. As we argued in Chapter
4, the conundrums of the researcher around success and failure
find their mirror image in the plight of social movements in
trying times. In what remains of this chapter, we want to see
if we can't recalibrate the ontology–epistemology–methodology

framework into a jury-rigged vehicle for social movement self-conceptualization, self-creation and self-management.

Opening time for the imagination

Throughout this book we've argued that social movements are driven by and co-create the radical imagination: shared landscapes of possibility and contestation that confront and contradict the reigning imaginaries of capital and power. We have argued that the radical imagination, in this sense, is not something individuals *have* but something networks, groups and movements *do*. More precisely, the radical imagination is something that both emerges from and guides collective doing. And yet, as we've argued, while movements are generating and being guided by the radical imagination, they are rarely self-conscious of the fact, at least not in any systematic way.

Indeed, one of the problems we noted over the course of our research (and that, in one way or another, most of our research participants confirmed) was that movements tend to get wrapped up in the day-to-day work of resisting systems of oppression and exploitation, focusing on tactical questions of how to 'get the job done', usually to the exclusion of the broader discussion of strategies to create change, let alone the principles and ideals that guide them, which exist in the shadow realm of the imagination. As we argued in Chapter 3, movements tend to create relatively few systems or structures to address these broader categories, and, as we argued in Chapter 6, this is all too often justified through recourse to motifs of time, urgency and efficacy (or lack thereof). The consequence of this, not infrequently, is the fragmentation or even shattering of movements over strategic issues, or due to the perpetuation of oppressive thematics or behaviours within movement spaces themselves. This is all the more the case in what we have called radical milieus (or, less flatteringly, what one of our participants indicted as 'scenes' or 'cliques') where the political landscape of contestation is made up of multiple overlapping groups, some permanent, some ad hoc, working on a variety of issues and that make common cause on particular initiatives. Here, the absence of any formal deliberative structure usually leads to an even *greater* fixation on day-to-day tactics, and while individual groups themselves might host retreats or discussions to reimagine broader issues, orientations and strategies, they almost never do so *together* (see Wood 2012). As a result, all too often discussion of goals, strategy, internal movement dynamics and oppression occurs either on the level of individual relationships, which lends itself to divisions and sects, or on the level of painfully obtuse abstraction (as we saw in Chapter 6), which lends itself to 'political correctness' and the abstraction of movement ideas and theories from their context.

Drawing out the threads of this conundrum, we suggest that a role for engaged researchers can be imagined as *opening the time* for the imagination and *opening spaces* for radical milieus to come together. In Chapter 4, we likened this to a form of radical 'therapy' that is about more than simply returning the 'patient' to some preordained 'normal' state and also about much more than just the expression of individual angst and self-pity (or self-castigation). And in Chapter 6 we spoke of the importance of *making time* for addressing movement dynamics (especially oppression) in order not merely to 'create a space' for diversity but to transform movement temporalities more broadly. Opening the time for the imagination means working with (and between) movements to break free of the tyranny of necessity and the day-to-day temporality of the struggle. It means to offer safe and positive (but not necessarily pleasant or unconfrontational) time to move beyond arguments about tactics and towards a clearer articulation of strategies and their guiding imaginaries. The goal is not to synchronize everyone's imagination to the universal revolutionary clock – it is not to produce agreement or consensus, although perhaps, through discussion, people might recognize their commonalities to a greater extent. As we have argued throughout this book, the radical imagination emerges from difference, contradiction and conflict, both within and between individuals, groups and movements. Rather, opening time for the radical imagination means creating a space for these tensions and differences to manifest themselves and to become tangible and powerful.

From imagination to strategy to tactics (and back)

Where do we look for a more systematic means to imagine the links between the broad imaginaries that animate radicalism, the particular political and strategic approaches that characterize different ideological positions and groups, and the day-to-day activities and tactics that so dominate the movement landscape? One possible answer to this vexing and complex question is to import the social research imagination model we outlined above. In so doing, we need to trade in three key phrases for the research imagination's triumvirate of ontology, epistemology and method: imagination, strategy and tactics. Like the research imagination model, these three align from the abstract

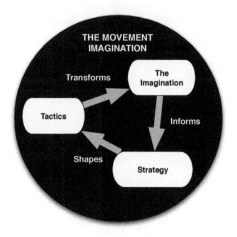

The movement imagination

to the concrete, from the general to the specific, although (as with ontology and method) imagination and tactics are also connected. Let's look at each in turn.

In our new triad, the imagination parallels the category of ontology. The imagination is a shared landscape and a common resource that both informs our actions and relationships and is, in turn, shaped by our actions and relationships. In this sense, the imagination is at once shared and individually possessed. The way we as individuals imagine ourselves and our relationship to the world around us is informed and incubated within our shared imaginaries. So aspects of the commonly imagined appear and resonate in the imaginations of particular individuals, but there can also be challenge, dissonance, disagreement and disparity: the radical imagination. For instance, as outlined in Chapter 4, queer liberation movements are, in part, individual and shared rejections of the overarching heteronormative imaginary which associates heterosexual relationships with nor-malcy and success and imagines as 'queer' all those behaviours, loves, relationships, desires and passions outside a narrowly defined set of social mores. Or, as we discussed above, the feminist radical imagination is built, in part, on the rejection of a patriarchal culture and belief system which privileges and exalts men and masculinized virtues.

Like ontology, the imagination is a way of interpreting and understanding social reality. Fundamentally, it is a shared framework for comprehending *difference*. That is, the imagi-nation is a means by which we seek to understand change, oddity, the unusual, the queer. Let's return to our hypothetical religious fundamentalist. His ontological understanding is that God is present on earth and has designed reality in his image, as laid out in scripture. He shares this imaginative framework with others in his congregation, his church and, more broadly, his religious tradition, and perhaps even with other religious traditions with which he doesn't otherwise agree (say, Jewish or Hindu fundamentalists). His sense of the world is, in this sense, both shared and his alone. This imaginary is not just a set of stories, ideas, rationalizations and doctrines. It is not a static thing. First, it is constantly being negotiated among all those who share the imaginary. Second, it is constantly being tested and challenged. So, if our religious fundamentalist's son or daughter tells him or her that he or she is gay, the fundamentalist's imaginary both provides a means to explain this 'difference' (by, say, rationalizing it as a Devil-inspired confusion which can be 'cured' through prayer) but is also shaken and strained by this encounter with difference. In other words, imaginaries are not explicit, fully articulated 'texts' out there to be read; they are living negotiations of identity, ideology, belief, understanding, theory, emotion, feeling and dreams that are activated not by unquestioning belief or doctrinaire ideology (although these, indeed, may be their manifestations) but by crisis, confusion, collision and compromise.

In this sense, imaginaries are the grounds for understanding social transformation. Throughout this book we have been using the idea of the 'radical imagination' to characterize those approaches that see social change as possible only outside the reigning social institutions. This gives us a sense of the way the imagination frames how we imagine history and society might change. It also ties it to the notion of ontology: what is the nature of social reality and, based on this, how can one change it? So, for instance, if one believes that social reality is made up of rational economic actors competing to survive, and that any form of government is simply the elevation of one competitive individual or group above the rest, then one might agree with F.A. Hayek (2009), Milton Friedman (2002), and others that a completely unfettered free market is best, and imagine that social change is a matter for individual economic actors. Likewise, if one imagined, along with many Marxists, that social reality is defined by the struggle between classes, and in particular the proletariat and the bourgeoisie, one might imagine that the pathway to social transformation depends on the mobilization of the proletariat towards the seizure of the means of production.

Before proceeding to strategy, a quick word regarding the difference between ideology and the imagination. For Marxist theorist Louis Althusser (1971: 162), ideology 'is a "representation" of the imaginary relationship of individuals to their real conditions of existence', one that can serve the interests of capital (when it occludes or misdirects our understanding of the world) or the interests of the proletariat (when it allows us to see larger, consistent patterns in social reality). This is a helpful definition, except that it implies a certain level of comprehensiveness and intentionality. In spite of the sophisticated theoretical work around the term by Althusser and others like Terry Eagleton (2007) that illustrates the confused, contradictory and mediated nature of ideological belief, the concept of 'ideology' still connotes a robust and self-contained suite of concepts and understandings with a clear and direct political orientation. We opt instead for the idea of the imagination in this framework to acknowledge the (perhaps lamentable) fact that the vast majority of social actors, and even social movement actors, are unable to articulate a clear, systematic ideological position. Most people's impressions of the social order and the potential to change it are a grab bag of ideas culled from books and other media, from those around them and from their own experience (see Taylor 2004). Even those individual scholars or movement intellectuals who have striven to develop a comprehensive ideological armature cannot be said to have totally synchronized their imaginations with an ideological position, simply because no ideology is ever fully complete – ideologies of all stripes are themselves constantly under negotiation and constantly encountering new social realities. Imaginaries are always slightly askew, slightly incomplete, always partial and conflicted, and the best ideologies accommodate and acknowledge this. By contrast, the most doctrinaire ideologies deny their own fallibility (e.g. fundamentalism, fascism) with disastrous consequences as, once empowered, they bend reality to fit the mould. To put this more systematically, the imagination is the target of ideologies. Ideologies offer, ultimately, a means to train or organize the imagination. The imagination is itself much more messy, complicated, contradictory and volatile.

Likewise, individuals can share common ideological tenets and yet have those animate and be animated by dramatically different imaginaries. For instance, under slavery in the US South, slavers and enslaved people often shared a common religion and heard the same doctrine, often from the same pulpit, yet the scripture often held completely different meanings for each. For the slavers, it was a justification of power; for the enslaved it was a source of inspiration and resistance (which is not to deny, too, that many white abolitionists were inspired by Christian doctrine, and many enslaved people were misguided by the slavers' imposed religion – see Hochschild 2006). Similarly, the various sects of Marxism and anarchism share a fidelity to certain key texts and ideas, but manifest as very different imaginaries. Hence the writings of Marx have been central to the imaginaries of Stalinism, Maoism, Liberation Theology, Autonomism, social democracy, and even certain forms of capitalist candour that admit the reality of class war but side with the current victors.

Imagination informs and guides strategy in much the same way that ontological assumptions inform epistemological approaches. How we imagine social relations and the possibilities for change will shape what sorts of broad strategies we believe might be effective. So, for instance, our aforementioned Marxist might agree with Lenin that the inherent basis of social relations is class struggle and the necessity of a proletarian uprising demands a centrally organized vanguard party that will deliver ideological unity and informed, committed leadership (Lenin 1902). The vanguardist strategy, in this case, stems directly from the way the social world is imagined. Similarly, if anarcho-primitivists imagine that social reality is based, fundamentally, on an unjust and unsustainable model of post-hunter–gatherer civilization, their strategy might be one of direct action against ecological destruction (such as 'eco-terrorism') or one of voluntary withdrawal from civilization to 'return' to what is imagined as a more authentic relationship to the land (Zerzan 2005). Things become more complicated in the vast majority of social movements, where the shared imaginary is less ideologically cohesive or coherent or where there are multiple strategies in play. We will come to these permutations in a moment. Strategies, then, are broader pathways for social transformation that collect within them more specific tactics and approaches. They can include commitments or aversions to certain types of tactics, organizational structures and imperatives, a perspective on building networks and alliances, and formal and informal modes of prestige and value for certain individuals and actions.

Tactics are the most concrete level of our model, the level that parallels 'method'. Tactics are the specific actions movements take to achieve their strategic objectives and can include kidnappings, petitions, activist film-making, public meetings, leafletting, protest marches and visioning sessions. Tactics represent discrete individual manoeuvres or actions that, taken together, constitute strategies.

This new triad of imagination–strategy–tactics helps us understand and explain a variety of phenomena we observed in our own research. Most social movement scholarship makes a few hasty assumptions, which we can plot through this framework. First and foremost, most researchers assume that each 'movement' is made up of relatively coherent, stable and self-contained groups that align on all three levels: their imagination leads to strategy; their strategy leads to tactics. But our argument here is that both individuals and groups are confused, contradictory, conflicted and co-creative on all these levels. One does not need to have a coherently articulated ideology that informs a fully thought-through strategy that inspires concrete tactics in order to act in the world. Individuals and groups between and within themselves are constantly struggling to bring these three levels into alignment. This is what allows individual activists to work in a variety of spheres. So, for instance, we interviewed many self-identified anarchists who actively and enthusiastically worked in social service organizations or environmental NGOs. They did so even though the imagination, strategy and tactics of anarchism and the social justice service sector are very different, and to a large extent opposed. We also spoke with union organizers who have well-refined and highly developed critiques of organized labour from a Marxist perspective, as well as supporters of social-democratic parties who engage in direct-action tactics when their more insurrectionary-minded comrades request their assistance and solidarity. Similarly, most activists with whom we spoke built their imaginations on the basis of the tactics that draw them to their respective movements. For instance, a number of people we interviewed talked about a strike, street demonstration or occupation as their introduction to the radical imagination. For them, a powerful encounter with a tactic in the context of a specific struggle or event grew into a sense of strategy and stimulated the imagination.

The triad of imagination–strategy–tactics is thus not a linear progression but a set of points on the horizon, some of which may seem nearer and clearer than others, but all of which are capable of constituting and feeding back upon one another. In advocating for a framework that highlights discontinuity, difference, confusion and dissonance we are advancing a research imagination capable of engaging living political milieus and the movements that inhabit them in all their dynamism and complexity.

Occupy

A good example of how confused the relationship between imagination–strategy–tactics can be in the context of living political struggles is the recent Occupy movement. In Halifax, Nova Scotia, as in many other cities, the Occupy movement was convened by a variety of actors with very different imaginaries. Initial meetings included union staffers, lifestyle anarchists, capitalist libertarians, members of social-democratic parties, back-to-the-land environmentalists, feminists (although many soon moved to the margins out of frustration), Indigenous solidarity activists, independent journalists, dyspeptic Marxist academics, and community members concerned with issues ranging from economic development to municipal animal control by-laws. As the movement evolved into regular meetings and an encampment outside City Hall in Halifax's downtown core, two processes saw a greater (but never complete) synchronization of the imagination. On the one hand, many of those at the margins drifted away, often frustrated with various dynamics of maintaining the occupation, negotiating with city officials and the police, as well as a variety of conflicts from the explicitly political to the interpersonal. On the other hand, for those who remained committed to the occupation, discussions and debates led to a greater imaginative synchronicity. This imaginative landscape, made up of multiple perspectives and approaches, was able to remain relatively unified around a shared *tactic*: the occupation of central urban space. For different activists, this tactic fed into different strategies. For some it was a means to draw media and broader public attention to the corrupt and unjust vicissitudes of the economic system. For others it was a space to recruit new members to political organizations. For still others, most of whom were unaffiliated and neophyte activists or activists whose communities were largely online, it was an opportunity to find like-minded individuals and have their conceptions of the status quo and the ways and means to change it challenged, affirmed or enriched through dialogue.

The tactic of occupation was a powerful and productive force for many new and established members of the Halifax activist community and it certainly seemed to provide fertile ground for the flowering of the radical imagination. At the same time, the centrality of the tactic of occupation to the reinvigoration of the radical imagination proved to be a significant weakness (see Khasnabish 2013). The location chosen for the Occupy encampment in Halifax was intended to be strategic. The Grand Parade – historic military parade grounds dating to the city's founding in the mid-1700s – is directly outside of Halifax City Hall, adjacent to the World Trade and Convention Centre, and the Toronto-Dominion Waterhouse bank main offices. The Cenotaph – a large standing sculpture commemorating Canadian soldiers killed in battle – stands at the centre of the grounds, and ultimately would provide a material and symbolic focal point for Occupy Nova Scotia's (Occupy NS) most significant political challenge. Initially, the rhetoric of municipal officials with respect to Occupy NS paid lip service to the spirit of civic engagement the occupiers supposedly represented. However, as the occupation wore on and Remembrance Day (a memorial day observed in Commonwealth countries since the end of World War I to commemorate members of national armed forces killed in war) drew nearer, the occupiers were increasingly drawn into a rhetorical dance with politicians and veterans about the ethics of their occupation, given the significance of the Grand Parade for Remembrance Day services. The symbolic significance of this tension in the context of Halifax, a long-time military town, cannot be overstated.

As the occupiers dealt, on the one hand, with the day-to-day struggles of reproducing life at the camp – including learning to negotiate internal tensions and working to integrate members struggling with mental health and substance-abuse issues – they also struggled publicly with the decision about whether or not to leave the Grand Parade. Ultimately, mobilizing language freighted with nationalism and militaristic patriotism, the occupiers declared they had reached a settlement with veterans and city officials. The Occupy NS camp would be temporarily relocated to another city park further west of the downtown core, the occupiers would take part in Remembrance Day memorial activities at Grand Parade, and the memorial activities would proceed as usual. On 11 November 2011, Remembrance Day, following the memorial ceremonies at the now unoccupied Grand Parade, Halifax Regional Police enacted a decision made in secret by the city council to forcibly evict the transplanted Occupy NS encampment mere hours after it had been established. The ensuing stand-off saw occupiers and their allies attempt to defend the new camp. While several occupiers were arrested, the resistance to the eviction was marred by disagreements over tactics and protocol. While the occupiers and their supporters would make a day-long symbolic return to Grand Parade a week after the Remembrance Day eviction and publicly denounce the perceived duplicity of city officials and the violence of the Halifax police force, the occupation was, to all intents and purposes, over.

The Remembrance Day eviction of Occupy NS and the events leading up to it shed critical light on the imagination–strategy–tactics triad that we've explored here. The tactic of occupation and its material manifestation revitalized the radical imagination for many new and established members of the Halifax activist milieu. At the same time, the centrality of the occupation in the imagination of its participants compromised Occupy NS in both the short and the longer term. In the short term, for members of Occupy NS, city politicians, the police and the broader public – supportive of the occupiers or not – the legitimacy and meaning of the occupation came to be interpreted through the lens of the space in which it occurred and the historical significance with which it is vested. Interestingly, the symbolic significance of Grand Parade and Remembrance Day cut both ways. On the one hand, Occupy NS was drawn, problematically and to the occupiers' distinct disadvantage, into a rhetorical and gestural affirmation of the patriotic, nationalistic and militaristic legacy embodied by Remembrance Day and the purposes it serves in the context of contemporary Canadian military adventurism. This not only diluted any radical critique of the status quo emanating from the camp; it also led ultimately to its violent eviction. On the other hand, given the widespread nationalist mythology that Canadian troops have always fought and died only for democracy, peace and justice (see McCready 2013; Razack 2004), when the mayor decided to use force to evict the occupiers on Remembrance Day in the midst of a rainstorm, public opinion turned significantly against the mayor and the city council. This was only exacerbated by the council's tradition of holding important discussions and taking decisions in private and without official minutes, thus rendering the operation of municipal power completely opaque to the public. Yet, in spite of the opening the eviction seemed to initially provide by exposing local political elites to sustained public scrutiny, this too was in the final instance reduced to a debate about the legality of urban camping, the use of off-the-record sessions at city council, and the latitude that ought to be afforded to protest, all rendered in a thoroughly liberal discourse that left little room for the radical imagination.

Over the longer term, Occupy NS had difficulty maintaining its life after its eviction. As with many other manifestations of the Occupy movement across the anglophone Atlantic, in the absence of a unifying tactic and the material site of the encampments, the remnants of the occupations found scant bases upon which to ground their strategic unity and longevity. In this sense, our triad model helps us illuminate the dangers of movements becoming too wedded to singular tactics, strategies and even imaginaries as such fealty denies innovation and adaptation, which are the bedrock of resilience. It also draws out the consequences of according tactics a place of privilege over and above strategic considerations and the imaginations that animate them. At the same time, both in Halifax and elsewhere, many activists found that their imaginations were more synchronized through the experience of working together and building and struggling to maintain the occupation tactic. Indeed, in the wake of Occupy NS's dissolution, this shared imaginative landscape gave rise to new networks and groups working on issues including solidarity with Indigenous protests, local food initiatives, anti-racist education, and more. This example reveals that, at a fundamental level, imaginations, strategies and tactics are in a dynamic and dialogic relationship that cannot be universally modelled or predicted. The triad model helps us break down and reimagine the way movements ebb and flow, clash and coincide, wax and wane, stagnate and transform.

Implications: 'diversity of tactics' as symptom

One might be tempted to conclude that if a model like this leads to so much confusion, it is of little analytical utility. But, as we have argued, this confusion is a social fact, not a consequence of our attempts to analyse and theorize it. Confusion and complexity are an important part of social movements and social life. Scholars have all too often sought out and valorized social movements that appear to be highly organized and ideologically coherent. But this is the case only for certain movements and only at particular moments in their lives. Coherence and organization are products of analytical attempts to make sense of movements rather than qualities inherent to them. Conventional analytical and theoretical attempts to make sense out of social movements are akin to taking snapshots. While they capture something of the phenomenon, they frame it, freeze it and separate it from the dynamic, living context in which it lives. If we are to assess the life of the radical imagination, we need to pay closer attention to the dissonance and the noise, the confusion and the contradiction, the joys and sorrows of the mess.

Of course, none of this is to say that these qualities are normative goods. Perhaps it is true, as most of our interviewees articulated, that a more unified and aligned paradigm would lead to more successful movements. Maybe this messiness, confusion and contradiction explain why movements tend not to sustain themselves over the long term and why they rarely achieve 'success' in the explicit terms they often set out for themselves. Perhaps this lack of coherence is part of a left culture that is, as some would claim, obsessed with failure (see Chapter 3). Certainly more robust theoretical and strategic groups (such as established socialist tendencies, trade unions and so on) tend to have greater institutional longevity. When there is a clearer alignment of imagination, strategy and tactics, it becomes easier for groups to pass on leadership, institutional resources and memory. But in describing radical milieus, we believe close attention to the messiness can be very valuable and demands exploration.

Our triad framework of imagination–strategy–tactics leads us to a few significant observations. First, 'successful' social movements tend to organize around shared strategies rather than shared imagination or shared tactics. That is, durable groups tend to congregate like-minded individuals based on a shared sense of the most powerful and efficacious pathways to create change. They can be made up of a diversity of activists who need not share the same imagination. For instance, an anti-poverty initiative aimed at providing information, advocacy and services to those experiencing homelessness can include anarchists, social democrats and Christian missionaries who have divergent and even contradictory imaginations regarding why poverty exists and why this particular strategy might be effective. Meanwhile, those who share a strategic approach need not share the same tactics. So, for instance, activist coalitions that organize to protest the visit of politicians or international trade meetings are usually made up of individuals and groups who agree that the best means to confront these forces is to network with other groups and stage several days of protest, where an infamous 'diversity of tactics' might be deployed. Of course, in both cases the breakdown of social movements and movement alliances is grounded in fissures along the lines of philosophical differences or tactical disagreements.

Our second observation is that key debates within and between movements tend to fixate on tactics. Based on our own research in this project and others, activist debates both online and offline are at their most contentious when they take up the question of what tactics are most effective at achieving desired ends and which ones threaten to fracture movement solidarity. As alluded to above, often such debates have circulated around the question of 'diversity of tactics' and the role of violence (or, more appropriately, property destruction) in protests. But they also revolve around participation in electoral processes, the utility of engaging with the mainstream media, and the way groups should be structured or meetings ought to be run.

Third, while they are least often articulated and debated, differences of imagination represent the most important and divisive fractures in and barriers to solidarity. Behind most debates about tactics and strategy a question of the imagination is at work. For instance, in the infamous 'diversity of tactics' debate, the anti-violence position is typically articulated by those who believe that the present structures of society (such as trade unions, NGOs and social-democratic political parties) are capable of transforming the system as a whole. In contrast, advocates of more vigorous tactics typically believe these institutions to be bankrupt barriers to change, and that destruction and violence are necessary parts of an insurgent consciousness. Other dimensions to this conflict of imagination are what constitutes 'violence' and what the significance of private property is within the social world. For many more liberal activists, smashing the window of a corporate storefront is both ineffective from a public outreach perspective and runs counter to the ethic of a movement striving to build a more just and peaceful world. For those who advocate for the utility of corporate property destruction and other confrontational tactics, it is the corporations themselves who are the truly violent ones as they ruin people, other life and the planet in their insatiable lust for profit. Furthermore, such radicals often contend, challenging power is not about media-friendly spectacle or bourgeois morality, much less about the sanctity of property; rather, it is about challenging the operations of the powerful in a direct and immanent way. Clearly, this debate is not about anything as simple as legality, tactics or even violence; it is about the very way these different actors imagine the stakes of the struggle at hand, the most successful routes to social change, and the nature of the dominant socio-political order itself.

Fourth, and more profoundly, dissonances of the imagination can take the form of the reproduction and invisibilization of oppression. All too often, we observed, the work of anti-oppression is marginalized and accorded a slot in the roster of revolutionary activity well below other priorities such as the transformation of the economic and political system. Confronting oppression is too often seen as a strategic fetish or a tactical matter: confronting racism, sexism and ableism, for example, comes to be seen as a matter of 'adding' these issues to the strategic agenda, or undertaking tactics like anti-oppression training or using inclusive language in pamphlets. In fact, the perpetuation of oppression in movements represents a foundational problem for the imagination. Those who do not suffer systematic oppression are largely unable (and often unwilling) to imagine its effects and dynamics, leading time and again to conflict and a breakdown in solidarity when strategies and tactics fail to address the deeper issues. As Marcel Stoetzler and Nira Yuval-Davis (2002) argue, the imagination is always situated by one's experience of oppression, exploitation, embodied privilege or abjection – it fundamentally shapes one's sense of the possible and one's perception of injustice. As we observed in Chapters 5 and 6, movements that fail to engage oppression critically and systematically (and its connections to exploitation and economic power) not only fail to challenge the dominant order effectively, they reproduce it.

EIGHT

Towards a prefigurative methodology

The framework we advance here is not intended simply to guide the research imagination of social movement scholars. It is also, we believe, a useful framework by which social movements can work on themselves, or by which researchers can begin to develop a constructive and progressive role in their engagements with movements. Throughout our interview process, we explicitly attempted to link the concrete to the abstract, asking questions of individuals and groups that sought to elicit how they linked imagination to strategy to tactics within their movements and milieus. As we have indicated, only rarely were any research participants able to articulate these links clearly, with many advancing a whole range of ideas and opinions only loosely connected to these categories. But one of the consistently positive responses we received from our participants, as we indicated in Chapter 2, was the affirmation that the opportunity to engage in critical, safe and reflexive dialogue, in a context that was neither instrumentally linked to organizing work nor politically competitive, was special and worthwhile. Social movements typically create very few individual and collective opportunities to lay bare beliefs, orientations, approaches, methods and doubts. Research can play a role in helping to make these ideas visible and common, or, alternately, to help sharpen and bring into focus the divisions, differences and dissonances that are the real substance of social movement milieus.

In future research, we can envisage developing the imagination–strategy–tactics framework into a set of participatory research workshops in the mode of the 'radical therapy' we articulated in Chapter 2. Such radical therapy would not be aimed at healing wounds and covering over discord, and so returning fragmented subjects to 'normal', but rather at developing a heightened awareness and reflexivity – among both movement participants and researchers – about these inherent dynamics without succumbing to hopelessness, despair, anger or frustration. That is, by working with movements to bring to the fore the often unstated (and perhaps even incoherent) linkages between imagination, strategy and tactics, we might create a new space for the radical imagination: a space where an awareness of difference can lead to new ideas, alliances, solidarities and possibilities.

How might that actually work? In the era of what scholars call 'new social movements' we have seen a gradual rise and adoption of so-called 'prefigurative politics'. Often, this notion is attributed to anarchist currents that are emergent and resurgent in the wake of the perceived failures of statist communism and socialism to deliver freedom, prosperity and equality in the Soviet Union, China and Cuba, and also the dreary and hierarchical atmospheres of Western communist parties since the middle of the twentieth century. Since the 1990s (and with antecedents in the New Left of the 1960s and 1970s), the idea that one's activism in the present would model or 'prefigure' the society one wants to build ('be the change' as the Gandhian slogan would have it) has arguably become the mainstream position in Western social movements, so much so that today some activists are averring neo-Leninisms in response, fixating on the (sometimes purely theoretical) need for more rigid organization and centralization.

While a focus on prefiguration can be dated back to the nineteenth-century anarchist tradition, where figures like Mikhail Bakunin insisted that the rejection of all authority and all bourgeois sensibilities was the hallmark of the true revolutionary (in contrast to more genteel, intellectual and vanguardist revolutionists, like Marx), such a story is distinctly limited. First, in the Western context, we can trace a prefigurative approach (for better or worse) to religious tendencies long before this, including the radical, millennialist Protestant uprisings of peasants and commoners throughout the Early Modern period, who believed in creating God's Kingdom of equality, justice and humility here on earth (Hill 1972; Linebaugh 2009). Or we can look to many of the Indigenous civilizations on Turtle Island (North America) and elsewhere for models of societies that were based on the principle that one's personal comportment and relationships were the bedrock of political reality (Akwesasne Notes 1978; Smith 2012). Second, we can note the many ways nineteenth-century (and even some later twentieth-century) anarchisms were clearly *not* prefigurative. For instance, the use of political violence – a practice known as 'propaganda by the deed' that marked some anarchist activity in the late nineteenth and early twentieth centuries – is clearly *not* a prefiguration of a future society, but a strategy aimed at creating the conditions whereby a new society might emerge (see Marshall 2010). Similarly, many strands of anarchism are (to our mind, rightly) distrustful of the sort of solipsistic and narcissistic individualism that can emerge from an exclusive focus on 'prefigurative' politics, which at their worst devolve into 'lifestyle politics' (Bookchin 2005). But, finally, associating prefigurative politics exclusively with the anarchist tradition is ahistorical, because in our view the present 'prefigurative turn' in contemporary radical politics owes much more to feminist, radical pacifist, anti-racist, queer and environmentalist activism, and is in fact a radical political thread that can be traced back centuries (see Epstein 1991; Federici 2003; Graham 2005, 2007, 2013; Linebaugh and Rediker 2000; Neigh 2012; Polletta 2002; Rediker 2004). While many of these other modern movements took inspiration, in part, from various forms of anarchism, and while each has contributed to the new anarchist forms that have become popular over the last three decades, it is important that, when we tell the story of the prefigurative turn, we highlight the centrality of these struggles to it.

For instance, much of today's activist focus on prefigurative approaches owes a debt to the feminist struggles surrounding the idea that 'the personal is the political', and the struggles of feminists within, against and beyond the patriarchal atmospheres of the New Left (Federici 2013; hooks 2000; James 2012; Rebick 2005; Weeks 2011). Indeed, even the emphasis on consensus, coalition-building, and egalitarian and horizontalist practices that marked the alter-globalization movement, particularly in the global North, as well as movements that have followed it, can be traced directly to the inspiration and dedicated work of radical and socialist feminists (see Ayres 1998; MacDonald 2002). Similarly, radical anti-racist activists like the Black Panthers were not simply interested in mobilizing a revolutionary cadre of black militants; they were also dedicated to changing the culture and social fabric of black communities, and, importantly, building alternative social structures of black valorization and survival against a white-supremacist economic, political, social and cultural landscape (Bloom and Martin 2013). Environmental activists quickly realized that a large part of their activism needed to be geared towards building sustainable alternatives to capitalist ecocide, ranging from personal consumer decisions to the establishment of alternative communities. And queer activists built their struggles around not merely political demands and a revolutionary horizon but the defence and cultivation of queer communities and identities (Kinsman and Gentile 2010; Warner 2005). In all these cases, struggles were, in whole or in part, grounded in a militant refusal of the reigning social imaginaries and demanded that both activists and allies behave and imagine themselves as citizens of a future community that had overcome oppression and exploitation. Renowned social movement scholar Alberto Melucci articulates the significance of the politics of prefiguration eloquently:

> People are offered the possibility of another experience of time, space, interpersonal relations, which opposes operational rationality of apparatuses. A different way of naming the world reverses the dominant codes. The medium, the movement itself as a new medium, is the message. As prophets without enchantment, contemporary movements practice in the present the change they are struggling for: they redefine the meaning of social action for the whole society. (1985: 801)

While perhaps too focused on the centrality of symbolic challenges to the dominant order as the site of movements' power, Melucci's comments allude poetically to the importance of the prefigurative turn, the roots of which lie much deeper than the recent anarchist revival and draw from soil much more diverse than the anarchist tradition – a tradition all too often associated with straight, male and white figureheads.

In any case, we agree with the many scholars who see the prefigurative turn as a key idiom of contemporary social movements (Day 2005). Indeed, almost all the participants with whom we spoke echoed, in whole or in part, the importance of a prefigurative approach. A few expressed scepticism towards the limits of prefigurative politics, arguing that a more disciplined and strategic approach was needed to actually transform systems of power. But even those who expressed such perspectives acknowledged the importance of developing revolutionary forms of relating to one another, movement structures, and economic, political, social and cultural institutions in the here and now as vital components of building a better world.

With this in mind, and thinking towards mobilizing the imagination–strategy–tactics framework we have outlined above, we want to trace the contours of what we imagine as a practice of 'prefigurative research'. Prefigurative research takes as its task imagining what 'research' might look like in a revolutionary world-to-come, bringing those forms, methods, ideas and orientations 'back' into the present. It demands we take seriously the challenge laid out by the feminist, anti-racist, environmental, queer and anarchist activisms: how can we build non-coercive, non-oppressive, non-hierarchal and non-exploitative relationships and institutions *today* that would be worthy exemplars of the world we want to create? What would a form of research look like that both modelled the future of 'research' in the world-to-come and also, crucially, aided and was an intimate part of struggles to bring that world into being?

We would have to begin with a key point, one that has been at work like a subterranean stream throughout this book but that it has come time to express directly. The future we wish to create does not include 'research' as we are accustomed to imagining it. Nor does it include the academy in its conventional form. In a society built on equality, opportunity, freedom, solidarity and possibility, the hierarchical, didactic, elitist and disconnected university will not only be an anachronism; it cannot exist. This is not to say that institutions of 'higher learning' would necessarily be done away with; nor that the universities of today are always and only pure spaces of oppression and domination. Rather, universities today are hybrid, conflicted spaces where different traditions and currents struggle with one another. When we speak of the autocratic, hierarchical, arrogant and detached university, we are speaking of perhaps the dominant contemporary thematic of the university, which so neatly (if miraculously) binds together, on the one hand, a patriarchal medieval guild system of elitist knowledge production and, on the other, radical new modes of neoliberal rationalization, including serving as the research and development wing for corporate capitalist profiteering, a reliance on the super-exploitation of precarious employees, and a cadre of corporate-style executives. While spaces can and do exist in all universities and in most departments for radical thinking, engaged and committed faculty and students, and responsibility to community, these are what Stefano Harney and Fred Moten (2103) call 'the undercommons', the commons of study and activism and relationship-building that exists perilously within increasingly rationalized and conservative institutional settings, but whose common labour and resources are, ironically, crucial to the university's functionality.

Within the paradigm of today's edu-factory, the ideals, objectives and methods of most research are clear: research exists to transform the world into functional knowledge. We can see this at work as 'unproductive' disciplines are either defunded or transformed. We can witness the way elements of a discipline like psychology have been rationalized into pseudosciences aimed at individualizing social pathologies and obeying the needs of the pharmaceuticals industry. We can see it in the ways that social-science programmes like anthropology and sociology have had their critical dimensions carefully culled, leaving behind technocratic training grounds for agents of the national security state – from prison guards to intelligence agents – domestically and abroad. Commitments to 'applied' and 'public' social research programmes have mushroomed over the last decade as the academy scrambles to answer not some genuine call to democratic engagement but the siren song of demonstrating its utility to the needs of political and economic elites. Even philosophy departments are increasingly turning to research and teaching in fields of 'applied ethics' or logic and analytic frameworks that lend themselves to military and corporate strategy. Those subdisciplines that resist corporate rationalization find themselves systematically impoverished, marginalized and even extinguished.

If the main purpose of today's university is the rationalization of research in the service of powerful vested interests, research on social movements is no exception. But who benefits? As we have outlined in Chapters 1 and 2, we are sceptical of most social movement research, much of which is oriented towards the generation of 'academic capital', has little responsibility to or resonance with social movements, is written in impenetrable specialized jargon, and is hidden away in esoteric academic journals. While some social movement scholars dedicate themselves to affirming and valorizing social movements through mainstream academic research and writing (what we have called a strategy of 'invocation'), we are not fully convinced that this is always particularly helpful, although there are some circumstances where it might be very helpful indeed. Similarly, we have spoken of scholars who put their research skills and academic privilege at the disposal of social movements, naming this a strategy of 'avocation'. And we have outlined our own strategy of 'convocation', where we attempt to occupy and mobilize the weird space of academic privilege to produce something new. While each is valuable in its own way and according to context, none is good enough to be a part of the future, better world we imagine and seek to build. This is where we must develop the concept of 'prefigurative' research.

So, in a future society what would research and universities look like? Much like our research participants when confronted with the question of what it would mean to win, our first response is a pregnant silence, a hiatus. A clear and singular response is difficult because we are the products of *this* oppressive, exploitative and unequal society, so our vision of the future will always be tainted. But we can make a few assumptions, although many of them are, regrettably, framed as negations of the present. And yet, as we noted in the Introduction, the radical imagination is not only a creative, shared facility; it is also a collective force that resists the status quo and refuses conscription. In this, it seeks to deny, disrupt and negate the current order just as much as it is the animating impulse of movements capable of remaking their worlds. We, too, are compelled to begin with what we hope is a creative negation: we can begin to glimpse the horizon of possibility through the critique and refusal of the present order.

So what possibilities can we glimpse for the university-to-come? For one, the university would cease to be the purveyor of commodified credentials. It may cease granting degrees altogether. It may instead become a place of retreat, discussion and study, but always in the service of community. This would not mean a sacrifice of academic freedom; it would, in fact, mean its expansion. Not only professional scholars would have the opportunity to engage in free and independent research, but all members of the community could enter and exit the university-to-come at different parts of their lives. It is likely that in a fair, just and solidarity-based society, we would do away with the 'profession' of the academic. While those with great academic talent may spend more time and energy in research and teaching, the guild-like monopoly would have to be abolished, and universities would need to be transformed into spaces where learning would not be top-down and didactic but where, in the spirit of Paolo Freire's (2000) 'pedagogy of the oppressed' and other advocates of de- and un-schooling (see Day, De Peuter and Coté 2007; Haworth 2012), the wall between the teacher and the learner is broken down. Within this framework, research in the sciences, medicine and engineering would continue, and of course certain individuals would need to assume leadership and be given the time and resources to engage in complicated research. The provision of resources for this research would cease to be the ad hoc chaos of corporate patronage but might come from a combination of arm's-length peer review and community and governmental support. The processes of research and learning will be radically democratized, along with the institutions and communities within which they will be embedded. In the process, the waste and drudgery of the current corporate university model will be abandoned and scholarship will become something truly relevant, engaging and worthwhile.

The case of the social sciences is more complicated. It is tempting to imagine it would be possible to build a world so free of social problems that the need for quantitative and qualitative research on society would be unnecessary, but this is an impossible utopia – akin to the 'top axis' in the diagrams in Chapter 2. The possible utopia is one where social research develops through a far more reflexive relationship. Today, the majority of social science orients itself, ultimately, towards informing policy. In so doing, the vast majority of it takes as given (and so further cements and reproduces) the dominant social, political, economic and cultural institutions and practices of our time. But in our vision of a different society, policy is not something imposed from the top down by educated bureaucrats, much less something that takes systems of exploitation and oppression as the natural backdrop for society for granted, but a living process grounded in radical grassroots democracy. That is, social goods like education, anti-violence initiatives, public health and justice would be grounded in community-based decision-making and implementation. This would necessarily demand a different form of social science, one that could stand slightly outside yet work in solidarity with communities. In this sense, social science would become a crucial organ or circuit of the constant work of community reproduction, a reflective apparatus or lens through which society could work on itself.

This is the heart of our imagining of 'prefigurative research': how can we build, in the here and now, a useful model of this sort of social science of the future? Key is the development of theoretical and discursive tools through which movements can *work on themselves* rather than being worked on by credentialled 'experts'. That is, prefigurative research should seek to work with movements to develop frameworks of reflexivity, self-creation and self-management. Rather than developing knowledge 'on' social movements (invocation) or knowledge 'for' social movements (avocation), a prefigurative research would, in the therapeutic mode outlined in Chapter 6, attempt to help movements develop knowledge of *themselves*. That is, it would work with movements and communities to develop ways of understanding, interpreting, identifying and working through the tensions, resonances, solidarities and failures they experience amidst their own reproduction.

It is for this reason that we have taken from the realm of academic research the model of ontology–epistemology–methods and transposed them with imagination–strategy–tactics. Prefigurative researchers can and should create circumstances and opportunities for activists and movements to reflect on, discuss, and work through each of these concepts and their relationships. Needless to say, there is no one-size-fits-all model for this. We are not seeking to build up a new paradigm with which to return to the academic mill and accumulate academic capital in endless, insular and largely irrelevant debates with others similarly disposed. What we offer here is one vision of what prefigurative research could look like and what it could do. The imagination–strategy–tactics framework we have outlined here is merely a sketch of nascent potential, a 'stem cell' from which many different organic forms might grow.

References

Albertani, Claudio. 2002. 'Paint It Black: Black Blocs, Tute Biance and Zapatistas in the Anti- Globalization Movement'. *New Political Science* 24 (4): 579–95.

Akwesasne Notes. 1978. *A Basic Call to Consciousness: the Haudenosaunee Address to the Western World*. Mohawk Nation: Akwesasne Notes.

Alexander, Michelle. 2010. *The New Jim Crow: Mass Incarceration in the Age of Colorblindness*. New York: The New Press.

Althusser, Louis. 2001. 'Ideology and Ideological State Apparatus (Notes Towards an Investigation)'. In *Lenin and Philosophy and Other Essays*, trans. Ben Brewster, pp. 85–126. New York: Monthly Review Press.

Anderson, Benedict. 2006. *Imagined Communities: Reflections on the Origin and Spread of Nationalism*. Rev. edn. London and New York: Verso.

Angell, Marcia. 2011. 'The Epidemic of Mental Illness: Why?' *New York Review of Books*, 23 June. www.nybooks.com/articles/archives/2011/jun/23/epidemic-mental-illness-why.

Appadurai, Arjun. 1996. *Modernity at Large: Cultural Dimensions of Globalization*. Minneapolis: University of Minnesota Press.

Armstrong, Jeannette, and Douglas Cardinal. 1991. *The Native Creative Process: A Collaborative Discourse*. Penticton BC: Theytus Books.

Atton, Chris. 2003. 'Infoshops in the Shadow of the State'. In J. Curran and Nick Couldry, eds, *Contesting Media Power: Alternative Media in a Networked World*, pp. 57–69. Lanham MD: Rowman & Littlefield.

Akwesasne Notes. 1978. *A Basic Call to Consciousness: The Haudenosaunee Address to the Western World*. Mohawk Nation: Akwesasne Notes.

Ayres, Jeffrey McKelvey. 1998. *Defying Conventional Wisdom: Political Movements and Popular Contention against North American Free Trade*. Studies in Comparative Political Economy and Public Policy. Toronto and Buffalo: University of Toronto Press.

Bagguley, Paul. 1992. 'Social Change, the Middle Class and the Emergence of "New Social Movements": A Critical Analysis'. *Sociological Review* 40 (February): 26–48.

Bakhtin, Mikhail. 1981. *The Dialogic Imagination: Four Essays*. Trans. Caryl Emerson and Michael Holquist. Austin: University of Texas Press.

Bandy, Joe, and Jackie Smith, eds. 2005. *Coalitions across Borders*. Lanham MD: Rowman & Littlefield.

Bannerji, Himani. 2000. *The Dark Side of the Nation: Essays of Multiculturalism, Nationalism and Gender*. Toronto: Canadian Scholars Press.

Benford, Robert, and David Snow. 1992. 'Master Frames and Cycles of Protest'. In Aldon Morris and Carol McClurg Mueller, eds, *Frontiers in Social Movement Theory*. New Haven CT: Yale University Press.

Berardi, Franco. 2009. 'Communism Is Back but We Should Call It the Therapy of Singularisation'. www.generation-online.org/p/fp_bifo6.htm.

Bishop, Anne. 2002. *Becoming an Ally: Breaking the Cycle of Oppression in People*. London: Zed Books and Halifax NS: Fernwood Publishing.

Blickstein, Susan, and Susan Hanson. 2001. 'Critical Mass: Forging a Politics of Sustainable Mobility in the Information Age'. *Transportation* 28: 347–62.

Bloom, Joshua, and Waldo E. Martin Jr. 2013. *Black Against Empire: The History and Politics of the Black Panther Party*. Berkeley, Los Angeles and London: University of California Press.

Blyth, Mark. 2013. *Austerity: The History of a Dangerous Idea*. Oxford and New York: Oxford University Press.

Bockmeyer, J. 2003. 'Devolution and the Transformation of Community Housing Activism'. *Social Science Journal* 40: 175–88.

Bookchin, Murray. 1995. *Social Anarchism or Lifestyle Anarchism: An Unbridgeable Chasm*. Oakland CA: AK Press.

Bourdieu, Pierre. 1984. *Distinction: A Social Critique of the Judgement of Taste*. Trans. Richard Nice. Cambridge MA: Harvard University Press.

Bousquet, Marc. 2008. *How the University Works: Higher Education and the Low-Wage Nation*. New York: New York University Press.

Brown, Wendy. 2010. *Walled States, Waning Sovereignty*. New York: Zone Books.

Buhle, Paul, and Nicole Schulman, eds. 2005. *Wobblies!: A Graphic History of the Industrial Workers of the World*. London and New York: Verso.

Butler, Judith. 1990. *Gender Trouble: Feminism and the Subversion of Identity*. New York and London: Routledge.

———. 2005. *Giving an Account of Oneself*. New York: Fordham University Press.

Caffentzis, George. 2013. *In Letters of Blood and Fire: Work, Machines, and the Crisis of Capitalism*. Oakland CA: PM Press.

Carlsson, Chris. 2010. 'Radical Patience: Feeling Effective over the Long Haul'. In Team Colors Collective, eds, *Uses of a Whirlwind: Movement, Movements, and Contemporary Radical Currents in the United States*, pp. 305–14. Oakland CA: AK Press.

Carroll, William K., and R.S. Ratner, eds. 2005. *Challenges and Perils: Social Democracy in Neoliberal Times*. Halifax NS: Fernwood Publishing.

Césaire, Aimé. 1972. *Discourse on Colonialism*. Trans. Joan Pinkham. New York and London: Monthly Review Press.

Christoff, Stefan. 2013. *Le Fond de l'Air est Rouge*. Montreal: Howl Arts Collective.

Clarke, Tony, and Canadian Centre for Policy Alternatives. 1997. *Silent Coup: Confronting the Big Business Takeover of Canada*. Toronto: James Lorimer.

Conway, Janet. 2004. *Identity, Place, Knowledge: Social Movements Contesting Globalization*. Halifax NS: Fernwood Publishing.

Couldry, Nick. 2010. *Why Voice Matters: Culture and Politics after Neoliberalism*. London and Thousand Oaks CA: Sage.

Crozier, Michel, Samuel P. Huntington, Joji Watanuki and Trilateral Commission. 1975. *The Crisis of Democracy: Report on the Governability of Democracies to the Trilateral Commission*. New York: New York University Press.

Davis, Lynne, ed. 2010. *Alliances: Re-envisioning Indigenous–Non-indigenous Relationships*. Toronto: University of Toronto Press.

Davis, Mike. 2006. *Planet of Slums*. London and New York: Verso.

Day, Richard. 2005. *Gramsci Is Dead: Anarchist Currents in the Newest Social Movements*. Toronto: Between the Lines.

Day, Richard, Greig De Peuter and Mark Coté, eds. 2007. *Utopian Pedagogy: Radical Experiments against Neoliberal Globalization*. Toronto: University of Toronto Press.

De Angelis, Massimo. 2007. *The Beginning of History: Value Struggles and Global Capital*. London: Pluto.

Dean, Jodi. 2012. *The Communist Horizon*. London and New York: Verso.

Della Porta, Donatella, Hanspeter Kriesi and Dieter Rucht. 2009. *Social Movements in a Globalizing World*. London and New York: Palgrave Macmillan.

Dyer-Witheford, Nick. 1999. *Cyber-Marx: Cycles and Circuits of Struggle in High-Technology Capitalism*. Urbana: University of Illinois Press.

Eagleton, Terry. 2007. *Ideology: An Introduction*. New edn. London and New York: Verso.

Edelman, Marc. 2001. 'Social Movements: Changing Paradigms and Forms of Politics'. *Annual Review of Anthropology* 30 (1) (October): 285–317.

Edu-factory Collective, ed. 2009. *Toward a Global Autonomous University: Cognitive Labor, the Production of Knowledge, and Exodus From the Education Factory*. New York: Autonomedia.

Ehrenreich, Barbara, and John Ehrenreich. 2013. 'The Real Story Behind the Crash and Burn of America's Managerial Class'. *AlterNet*, 19 February. www.alternet.org/economy/barbara-and-john-ehrenreich-real-story-behind-crash-and-burn-americas-managerial-class?paging=off.

Epstein, Barbara. 1991. *Political Protest and Cultural Revolution: Nonviolent Direct Action in the 1970s and 1980s*. Berkeley: University of California Press.

Farrow, Heather, Pam Moss and Barbara Shaw. 1995. 'Symposium on Feminist Participatory Research'. *Antipode* 27 (1): 77–101.

Featherstone, David. 2012. *Solidarity: Hidden Histories and Geographies of Internationalism*. London: Zed Books.

Federici, Silvia. 2003. *Caliban and the Witch: Women, the Body and Primitive Accumulation*. New York: Autonomedia and London: Pluto.

———. 2012. *Revolution at Point Zero: Housework, Reproduction, and Feminist Struggle*. Oakland CA: PM Press.

Femion, Yves. 2002. *Orgasms of History: 3000 Years of Spontaneous Insurrection*. Oakland CA: AK Press.

Fish, Stanley. 1997. 'Boutique Multiculturalism, or Why Liberals Are Incapable of Thinking about Hate Speech'. *Critical Inquiry* 23 (2): 378.

Fisher, Mark. 2009. *Capitalist Realism: Is There No Alternative?* London: Zero Books.

Foster, John Bellamy, Brett Clark and Richard York. 2010. *The Ecological Rift: Capitalism's War on the Earth*. New York: Monthly Review Press.

Fraser, Nancy. 2013. *Fortunes of Feminism: From State-Managed Capitalism to Neoliberal Crisis*. London and New York: Verso.

Freire, Paulo. 2000. *Pedagogy of the Oppressed*. 30th anniversary edn. New York: Continuum.

Friedman, Milton. 2002. *Capitalism and Freedom*. 40th anniversary edn. Chicago and London: University of Chicago Press.

Giroux, Henry. 2004. *The Terror of Neoliberalism*. Boulder CO: Paradigm.

———. 2012. *Disposable Youth, Racialized Memories, and the Culture of Cruelty*. London and New York: Routledge.

Goodwin, Jeff, James Jasper and Francesca Polletta. 2001. *Passionate Politics: Emotions and Social Movements*. Chicago: University of Chicago Press.

Gordon, Linda. 2002. 'Social Movements, Leadership, and Democracy: Toward More Utopian Mistakes'. *Journal of Women's History* 14: 102–17.

Graeber, David. 2001. *Toward an Anthropological Theory of Value: The False Coin of Our Own Dreams*. London and New York: Palgrave Macmillan.

———. 2002. 'The New Anarchists'. *New Left Review* 13: 61–73.

———. 2007. *Possibilities: Essays on Hierarchy, Rebellion, and Desire*. Oakland CA.

———. 2009. *Direct Action: An Ethnography*. Oakland CA: AK Press.

———. 2011. 'Occupy Wall Street Rediscovers the Radical Imagination'. *Guardian*, 25 September. www.guardian.co.uk/commentisfree/cifamerica/2011/sep/25/occupy-wall-street-protest.

Graham, Robert, ed. 2005. *Anarchism: A Documentary History of Libertarian Ideas*, vol. 1. Montreal and New York: Black Rose Books.

———, ed. 2007. *Anarchism: A Documentary History of Libertarian Ideas*, vol. 2. Montreal and New York: Black Rose Books.

———, ed. 2013. *Anarchism: A Documentary History of Libertarian Ideas*, vol. 3. Montreal and New York: Black Rose Books.

Haiven, Max. 2014. *Crises of Imagination, Crises of Power: Capitalism, Creativity and the Commons*. London: Zed Books.

———. 2011a. 'Undead Ideologies: Necro-Neoliberalism, Necro-Keynesianism and the Radical Imagination'. *ZNet*. www.zcommunications.org/

undead-ideologies-necro-neoliberalism-necro-keynesianism-and-the-radical-imagination-by-max-haiven.

———. 2011b. 'Are Your Children Old Enough to Learn About May '68? Recalling the Radical Event, Refracting Utopia, and Commoning Memory'. *Cultural Critique* 78 (1): 60–87.

Haiven, Max, and Alex Khasnabish. 2010. 'What Is Radial Imagination? A Special Issue'. *Affinities: A Journal of Radical Theory, Culture, and Action* 4 (2): i–xxxvii.

Halberstam, Judith. 2011. *The Queer Art of Failure*. Durham NC: Duke University Press.

Harding, Sandra G., ed. 2004. *The Feminist Standpoint Theory Reader: Intellectual and Political Controversies*. New York: Routledge.

Hardt, Michael, and Antonio Negri. 2000. *Empire*. Cambridge MA: Harvard University Press.

———. 2004. *Multitude: War and Democracy in the Age of Empire*. New York: Penguin.

———. 2011. *Commonwealth*. Cambridge MA: Belknap Press of Harvard University Press.

Hardt, Michael, and Paolo Virno, ed. 1996. *Radical Thought in Italy: A Potential Politics*. Minneapolis: University of Minnesota Press.

Harney, Stefano, and Fred Moten. 2013. *The Undercommons: Fugitive Planning & Black Study*. Brooklyn and Wivenhoe: Minor Compositions.

Harvey, David. 2003. *The New Imperialism*. Oxford: Oxford University Press.

———. 2006. *The Limits to Capital*. 2nd edn. London and New York: Verso.

Haworth, Robert H., ed. 2012. *Anarchist Pedagogies: Collective Actions, Theories, and Critical Reflections on Education*. Oakland CA: PM Press.

Hayek, F A. 2009. *The Road to Serfdom: Text and Documents*. Ed. Bruce Caldwell. Chicago and London: University of Chicago Press.

Hedges, Chris. 2010. *The Death of the Liberal Class*. Toronto: Alfred A. Knopf.

———. 2013. *The World as It Is: Dispatches on the Myth of Human Progress*. New York: Nation Books.

Hedges, Chris, and Joe Sacco. 2012. *Days of Destruction, Days of Revolt*. Toronto: Knopf.

Hesse-Biber, Sharlene Nagy, ed. 2012. *Handbook of Feminist Research: Theory and Praxis*. 2nd edn. London and Thousand Oaks CA: Sage.

Hill, Christopher. 1972. *The World Turned Upside Down: Radical Ideas during the English Revolution*. London and New York: Penguin.

Holloway, John. 2002. *Change the World without Taking Power: The Meaning of Revolution Today*. London: Pluto Press.

Hochschild, Adam. 2006. *Bury the Chains: Prophets and Rebels in the Fight to Free an Empire's Slaves*. New York: Mariner.

hooks, bell. 2000. *Feminism Is for Everybody: Passionate Politics*. Cambridge MA: South End Press.

Huyer, Sophia. 2004. 'Challenging Relations: A labour–NGO Coalition to Oppose the Canada–US and North American Free Trade Agreements, 1985–1993'. *Development in Practice* 14 (1–2) (February): 48–60.

James, Selma. 2012. *Sex, Race, and Class: The Perspective of Winning*. Brooklyn NY: Common Notions (PM Press).

Jameson, Fredric. 1976. 'Foreword'. In *On Meaning: Selected Writings in Semiotic Theory*, ed. Algirdas Greimas, trans. Paul J. Perron and Frank H. Collins. Minneapolis and London: University of Minnesota Press.

———. 1981. *The Political Unconscious*. Ithaca NY: Cornell University Press.

Jasper, James. 1999. *The Art of Moral Protest: Culture, Biography, and Creativity in Social Movements*. Chicago: University of Chicago Press.

Juris, Jeffrey S. 2008. *Networking Futures: The Movements against Corporate Globalization*. Durham NC and London: Duke University Press.

Juris, Jeffrey S., and Alex Khasnabish, eds. 2013. *Insurgent Encounters: Transnational Activism, Ethnography, and the Political*. Durham NC and London: Duke University Press.

Katsiaficas, George. 1987. *The Imagination of the New Left: A Global Analysis of 1968*. Boston MA: South End Press.

———. 2006. *The Subversion of Politics: European Autonomous Social Movements and the Decolonization of Everyday Life*. Oakland CA: AK Press.

Keck, Margaret, and Kathryn Sikkink. 1998. *Activists beyond Borders: Advocacy Networks in International Politics*. Ithaca NY: Cornell University Press.

Keefer, Tom. 2007. 'The Politics of Solidarity: Six Nations, Leadership, and the Settler Left'. *Upping the Anti: A Journal of Theory and Action* 4: 107–23.

Kelley, Robin. 2002. *Freedom Dreams: The Black Radical Imagination*. Boston MA: Beacon Press.

Khasnabish, Alex. 2008. *Zapatismo beyond Borders: New Imaginations of Political Possibility*. Toronto: University of Toronto Press.

———. 2013. 'Occupy Nova Scotia: The Symbolism and Politics of Space'. *Fieldsights – Hot Spots, Cultural Anthropology Online*. http://culanth.org/fieldsights/91–occupy-nova-scotia-the-symbolism-and-politics-of-space.

Khasnabish, Alex, and Max Haiven. 2012. 'Convoking the Radical Imagination: Social Movement Research, Dialogic Methodologies, and Scholarly Vocations'. *Cultural Studies <–> Critical Methodologies* 12 (5) (July): 408–21.

Kidd, Dorothy. 2003. 'The Independent Media Center: A New Model'. *Media Development* 50 (4): 7–11.

Klein, Naomi. 2008. *The Shock Doctrine: The Rise of Disaster Capitalism*. Toronto: Vintage Canada.

Lacey, A. 2005. 'Networked Communities: Social Centers and Activist Spaces in Contemporary Britain'. *Space and Culture* 8 (1 August): 286–301.

Lal, Vinay. 2002. *Empire of Knowledge: Culture and Plurality in the Global Economy*. London: Pluto Press.

Léger, Marc James. 2013. *The Neoliberal Undead: Essays on Contemporary Art and Politics*. London: Zero.

Lenin, V.I. 1902. *What Is to Be Done?* Trans. Joe Fineberg and George Hanna. The Marxist Internet Archive. www.marxists.org/archive/lenin/works/1901/witbd.

Levine, Bruce E. 2013. 'Why Life in America Can Literally Drive You Insane'. *AlterNet*, 30 July. www.alternet.org/personal-health/whats-behind-dramatic-rise-mental-illness?akid=10746.157687.IjW1wd&rd=1&src=news letter876072&t=3&paging=off.

Lewontin, Richard. 1996. *Biology as Ideology: The Doctrine of DNA*. Toronto: House of Anansi Press.

Linebaugh, Peter. 2009. *The Magna Carta Manifesto: Liberties and Commons for All*. Berkeley CA: University of California Press.

Linebaugh, Peter, and Marcus Rediker. 2000. *The Many-headed Hydra: Sailors, Slaves, Commoners, and the Hidden History of the Revolutionary Atlantic*. Boston MA: Beacon Press.

Loewe, B. 2012. 'An End to Self-Care'. *Organizing Upgrade*. 15 October. www.organizingupgrade.com/index.php/modules-menu/community-care/item/731-an-end-to-self-care-|-b-loewe.

Lorde, Audre. 1988. *A Burst of Light*. Ithaca NY: Firebrand Books.

Lowry, Michelle, and Peter Nyers. 2003. 'Roundtable Report "No One Is Illegal": The Fight for Refugee and Migrant Rights in Canada'. *Refuge* 21 (3): 66–72.

Luxemburg, Rosa. 2003. *The Accumulation of Capital*. London and New York: Routledge.

Lynd, Staughton, and Andrej Grubačić. 2008. *Wobblies & Zapatistas: Conversations on Anarchism, Marxism and Radical History*. Oakland CA: PM Press.

MacDonald, Laura. 2002. 'Globalization and Social Movements: Comparing Women's Movements Responses to NAFTA in Mexico, the USA and Canada'. *International Feminist Journal of Politics* 4 (2) (January): 151–72.

Maeckelbergh, Marianne. 2009. *The Will of the Many*. London: Pluto Press.

Maguire, Patricia. 1996. 'Considering More Feminist Participatory Research'. *Qualitative Inquiry* 2: 106–19.

Mansbridge, Jane, and Aldon Morris, eds. 2001. *Oppositional Consciousness: The Subjective Roots of Social Protest*. Chicago: University of Chicago Press.

Martin, Randy. 2011. *Under New Management: Universities, Administrative Labor, and the Professional Turn*. Philadelphia: Temple University Press.

Martínez, Elizabeth Betita. 2000. 'Where Was the Color in Seattle? Looking for Reasons Why the Great Battle Was So White'. *Colorlines*. 10 March. http://colorlines.com/archives/2000/03/where_was_the_color_in_seattlelooking_for_reasons_why_the_great_battle_was_so_white.html.

Marshall, Peter. 2010. *Demanding the Impossible: A History of Anarchism*. Oakland CA: PM Press.

Marx, Karl. 1992. *Capital I: A Critique of Political Economy*. New York: Penguin.

Marx, Karl, and Friedrich Engels. 2004. *The Communist Manifesto*. Ed. Len Findlay. Peterborough ON: Broadview.

McBride, Stephen. 2005. '"If You Don't Know Where You're Going You'll End up Somewhere Else": Ideological and Policy Failure in the Ontario NDP'. In William K. Carroll and R.S. Ratner, eds, *Challenges and Perils: Social Democracy in Neoliberal Times*. Halifax NS: Fernwood Publishing.

McCready, A.L. 2013. *Yellow Ribbons: The Militarization of National Identity in Canada*. Halifax NS: Fernwood Publishing.

McKay, Ian. 2005. *Rebels, Reds, Radicals: Rethinking Canada's Left History*. Toronto: Between the Lines.

McMurtry, John. 2013. *The Cancer Stage of Capitalism: From Crisis to Cure*. London: Pluto.

McNally, David. 2011. *Global Slump: The Economics and Politics of Crisis and Resistance*. Oakland CA: PM Press.

Melucci, Alberto. 1985. 'The Symbolic Challenge of Contemporary Movements'. *Social Research* 52 (4): 789–816.

Midnight Notes Collective. 1992. *Midnight Oil: Work, Energy, War, 1973-1992*. Brooklyn NY: Autonomedia.

Mies, Maria. 1986. *Patriarchy and Accumulation on a World Scale: Women in the International Division of Labour*. London: Zed Books.

Mohanty, Chandra Talpade. 2003. *Feminism without Borders: Decolonizing Theory, Practicing Solidarity*. Durham NC and London: Duke University Press.

'National Intimate Partner and Sexual Violence Survey'. 2011. Atlanta GA: National Center for Injury Prevention and Control, Centers for Disease Control and Prevention.

Neigh, Scott. 2012. *Resisting the State: Canadian History through the Stories of Activists*. Halifax NS: Fernwood Publishing.

Network of Concerned Anthropologists, ed. 2009. *The Counter-Counter-insurgency Manual: Or, Notes on Demilitarizing American Society*. Chicago IL: Prickly Paradigm Press.

Olesen, Thomas. 2005. *International Zapatismo: The Construction of Solidarity in the Age of Globalization*. London: Zed Books.

Osterweil, Michal. 2010. '"Becoming-Woman?" In Theory or in Practice'. In Turbulence Collective, ed., *What Would It Mean to Win?*, pp. 82–9. Oakland CA: PM Press.

Padamsee, Yashna. 2011. 'Communities of Care'. *Organizing Upgrade*. 1 July. www.organizingupgrade.com/index.php/component/k2/item/88-yashna-communities-of-care.

Passerini, Luisa. 1996. *Autobiography of a Generation: Italy, 1968*. Hanover and London: Wesleyan University Press.

Paulson, Justin. 2010. 'The Uneven Development of Radical Imagination'. *Affinities: A Journal of Radical Theory, Culture, and Action* 4 (2): 33–8.

Perelman, Michael. 1987. *Marx's Crisis Theory: Scarcity, Labour and Finance.* New York and London: Praeger.

———. 2000. *The Invention of Capitalism: Classical Political Economy and the Secret History of Primitive Accumulation.* Durham NC and London: Duke University Press.

Philip, M. Nourbese. 1992. *Frontiers: Selected Essays and Writings on Racism and Culture, 1984–1992.* Stratford ON: Mercury Press.

Pickard, Victor W. 2006. 'Assessing the Radical Democracy of Indymedia: Discursive, Technical, and Institutional Constructions'. *Critical Studies in Media Communication* 23 (March): 19–38.

Plyler, Jen. 2006. 'How to Keep on Keeping on: Sustaining Ourselves in Community Organizing and Social Justive Struggles'. *Upping the Anti: A Journal of Theory and Action* 3: 123–34.

Polletta, Francesca. 2002. *Freedom Is an Endless Meeting: Democracy in American Social Movements.* Chicago: University of Chicago Press.

Prashad, Vijay. 2007. *The Darker Nations: A People's History of the Third World.* New York and London: New Press.

———. 2013. *The Poorer Nations: A Possible History of the Global South.* London and New York: Verso.

Price, David H. 2011. *Weaponizing Anthropology: Social Science in Service of the Militarized State.* Oakland CA: AK Press.

Razack, Sherene. 2008. *Casting Out: The Eviction of Muslims From Western Law and Politics.* Toronto: University of Toronto Press.

———. 2004. *Dark Threats, White Knights: The Somalia Affair, Peacekeeping, and the New Imperialism.* Toronto: University of Toronto Press.

Read, Jason. 2003. 'What Is Living and What Is Dead in the Philosophy of Karl Marx: The Political Ontology of Living Labor'. In *The Micro-Politics of Capital*, pp. 61–102. Albany NY: SUNY Press.

Rebick, Judy. 2005. *Ten Thousand Roses: The Making of a Feminist Revolution.* Toronto: Penguin Canada.

Rediker, Marcus. 2004. *Villains of All Nations: Atlantic Pirates in the Golden Age.* Boston MA: Beacon Press.

———. 2007. *The Slave Ship: A Human History.* New York: Viking.

Reinsborough, Patrick. 2010. 'Giant Whispers: Narrative Power, Radical Imagination and a Future Worth Fighting for'. *Affinities: A Journal of Radical Theory, Culture, and Action* 4 (2): 67–78.

Roggero, Gigi. 2011. *The Production of Living Knowledge: The Crisis of the University and the Transformation of Labor in Europe and North America.* Trans. Enda Brophy. Philadelphia PA: Temple University Press.

Ross, Kristin. 2002. *May '68 and Its Afterlives.* Chicago: University of Chicago Press.

Selbin, Eric. 2010. *Revolution, Rebellion, Resistance: The Power of Story.* London: Zed Books.

Shiva, Vandana. 1997. *Biopiracy: The Plunder of Nature and Knowledge*. Boston MA: South End Press.

Shotwell, Alexis. 2011. *Knowing Otherwise: Race, Gender, and Implicit Understanding*. State College PA: Penn State University Press.

Shukaitis, Stephen, David Graeber and Erika Biddle, eds. 2007. *Constituent Imagination*. Oakland CA: AK Press.

Sinclair, Scott, and John Jacobs. 2007. *Atlantica Myths and Realities*. Ottawa: CCPA.

Sitrin, Marina. 2012. *Everyday Revolutions: Horizontalism and Autonomy in Argentina*. London: Zed Books.

Sivanandan, Ambalavaner. 1990. *Communities of Resistance: Writings on Black Struggles for Socialism*. London and New York: Verso.

Smith, Andrea. 2005. *Conquest: Sexual Violence and American Indian Genocide*. Cambridge MA: South End Press.

Smith, Linda Tuhiwai. 2012. *Decolonizing Methodologies: Research and Indigenous Peoples*. London: Zed Books.

Solnit, David, ed. 2004. *Globalize Liberation: How to Uproot the System and Build a Better World*. San Francisco: City Lights Books.

Staggenborg, Suzanne. 2012. *Social Movements*. Oxford: Oxford University Press.

Stoetzler, M., and N. Yuval-Davis. 2002. 'Standpoint Theory, Situated Knowledge and the Situated Imagination'. *Feminist Theory* 3 (December): 315–33.

Stuckler, David, and Sanjay Basu. 2013. *The Body Economic: Why Austerity Kills*. New York: HarperCollins.

Tarrow, Sidney. 1988. 'National Politics and Collective Action: Recent Theory and Research in Western Europe and the United States'. *Annual Review of Sociology* 14: 421–40.

———. 2005. *The New Transnational Activism*. Cambridge and New York: Cambridge University Press.

Taylor, Astra. 2013. 'From the Ashes of Occupy: On Failing Better and Erasing Debts'. *Hazlitt*, 14 November. www.randomhouse.ca/hazlitt/feature/ashes-occupy-failing-better-and-erasing-debts.

Taylor, Charles. 2004. *Modern Social Imaginaries*. Durham NC and London: Duke University Press.

Thompson, A.K. 2010. *Black Bloc, White Riot: Anti-Globalization and the Genealogy of Dissent*. Oakland CA: AK Press.

Thompson, E.P. 1968. *The Making of the English Working Class*. New York: Pantheon Books.

Thorburn, Elise. 2012. 'Squarely in the Red: Dispatches from the 2012 Quebec Student Strike'. *Upping the Anti: A Journal of Theory and Action* 14: 107–21.

Touraine, Alain. 2002. 'The Importance of Social Movements'. *Social Movement Studies* 1 (1) (April): 89–95.

Turbulence Collective. 2010. *What Would It Mean to Win?* Oakland CA: PM Press.

Urribarri, Fernando. 2002. 'Castoriadis: The Radical Imagination and the Post-Lacanian Unconscious'. *Thesis Eleven* 71 (1): 40–51.

Virno, Paolo. 2003. *A Grammar of the Multitude: For an Analysis of Contemporary Forms of Life*. Semiotext(e) Foreign Agents Series. Cambridge MA and London: Semiotext(e).

Wachsmuth, David, and Shiri Pasternak. 2008. 'Use It or Lose It: Toronto's "Abandonment Issues" Campaign for Affordable Housing'. *Critical Planning* 15: 7–21.

Walia, Harsha. 2013. *Undoing Border Imperialism*. Oakland CA: AK Press and the Institute for Anarchist Studies.

Wallerstein, Immanuel. 1996. *Open the Social Sciences: Report of the Gulbenkian Commission on the Restructuring of the Social Sciences*. Stanford CA: Stanford University Press.

Warner, Michael. 2005. *Publics and Counterpublics*. New York: Zone Books.

Warnock, Peter. 2005. 'The CCF–NDP in Saskatchewan: From Populist Social Democracy to Neoliberalism'. In William K. Carroll and R.S. Ratner, eds, *Challenges and Perils: Social Democracy in Neoliberal Times*. Halifax NS: Fernwood Publishing.

Weeks, Kathi. 2011. *The Problem with Work: Feminism, Marxism, Antiwork Politics, and Postwork Imaginaries*. Durham NC and London: Duke University Press.

Williams, Jeffrey J. 2008. 'Student Debt and the Spirit of Indenture'. *Dissent* 55 (4): 73–8.

Wilson, Shawn. 2009. *Research Is Ceremony: Indigenous Research Methods*. Halifax NS: Fernwood Publishing.

Wood, Lesley J. 2012. *Direct Action, Deliberation, and Diffusion: Collective Action after the WTO Protests in Seattle*. Cambridge: Cambridge University Press.

Wright, Steve. 2002. *Storming Heaven: Class Composition and Struggle in Italian Autonomist Marxism*. London: Pluto.

Zerzan, John. 2005. *Against Civilization: Readings and Reflections*. Port Townsend WA: Feral House.

Index